T0195261

THE OLD ONES IN THE OLD BOOK

Much of what we thought we knew about the Old Testament is here challenged in a most interesting and provocative way.
Richard Coggins, formerly Senior Lecturer in Old Testament Studies at King's College London, and author of *Introducing the Old Testament*.

An important and timely book, which everyone concerned with spirituality in our time should read.
John Matthews, author of *The Western Way*

Readers will find in Phil West's very readable book a distillation of a century of scholarship on the different ways in which the beliefs of surrounding cultures played a key part in the emergence of what we now know as the Hebrew Bible.
Christopher Rowland, Dean Ireland's Professor of the Exegesis of Holy Scripture, University of Oxford.

West has excelled in making academic standard research into a fascinating and exciting read. This book should be of interest to Jews, Christians, Pagans and readers generally interested in the development of spiritual paths, and become a handy reference source for years to come.
Pete Jennings, past President of The Pagan Federation and author of *Pagan Paths*.

With a style that's a pleasure to read, Philip West shares the best of Old Testament scholarship revealing what is common knowledge in academia but largely unknown in the public arena – the profound influence of the pagan Canaanite religion on the evolution, practices and sacred writings of Judaism and Christianity. Reasoned and revolutionary, an important book and a must read.

Phyllis Curott, attorney, author of *Book of Shadows*, Wiccan Priestess, and Trustee of the Council for the Parliament of the World's Religions.

The Old Ones in the Old Book

Pagan Roots of the
Hebrew Old Testament

The Old Ones in the Old Book

Pagan Roots of the Hebrew Old Testament

Philip West

Winchester, UK
Washington, USA

First published by Moon Books, 2012
Moon Books is an imprint of John Hunt Publishing Ltd., Laurel House, Station Approach,
Alresford, Hants, SO24 9JH, UK
office1@o-books.net
www.o-books.com

For distributor details and how to order please visit the 'Ordering' section on our website.

Text copyright: Philip West 2011

ISBN: 978 1 78099 171 9

A CIP catalogue record for this book is available from the British Library.

Design: Stuart Davies

Printed and bound by CPI Group (UK) Ltd, Croydon, CR0 4YY
Printed in the USA by Offset Paperback Mfrs, Inc

We operate a distinctive and ethical publishing philosophy in all
areas of our business, from our global network of authors to
production and worldwide distribution.

CONTENTS

Preface   1

Maps   3

1. Introduction   4

What is the Old Testament?   5

The significance of the Old Testament

The official plot of the Old Testament   7

The reality underneath   9

A note on translations, footnotes and paganism

2. The Religion of the Patriarchs   11

The official version: Abraham the first worshiper of Yahweh

Who were the patriarchs?   12

The gods of the patriarchs   13

El

The Canaanite high god   14

The gods of the fathers

The gods of the local shrines   15

Conclusion

Individual stories of encounters with the divine   16

Three divine figures by the Oaks of Mamre

Jacob's ladder   17

Wrestling with a god   18

3. Yahweh, Mount Sinai and Moses   21

The official version: Yahweh as the only true God

Yahweh, Midian and Sinai   22

Yahweh's home   23

The Song of Deborah   24

Elijah at Horeb   25

Yahweh: a distinctive god   26

Magic in the Moses traditions   28
Moses' rod   29
Battle with the Amalekites   31
The bronze serpent   32
The circumcision of Moses' son   33
The escape from Egypt
The Passover night   34
Deliverance at the Red Sea   35
The Covenant at Sinai   37
The Ten Commandments   38
The golden calf   40

4. Religion in Canaan before King David   42
The official version: the revealed religion of Sinai
What actually happened   43
The evidence from Ugarit   44
The Canaanite gods
The poetic myths   46
The Canaanite cult
Israelite and Canaanite religion   47
El   48
Baal   49
The cult   50
Divination   52
Human sacrifice   54
The ark   55

5. Jerusalem, King and Temple   57
The official version: David the fulfillment of
    Yahweh's vision
David and the capture of Jerusalem   58
Sacral kingship   59
Zion   60
The priesthood   61

David and Solomon

Marriage, religion and politics 63

Solomon's Temple 64

Conclusion 67

6. Divided Kingdoms and Hebrew Goddesses 68

The official version: Israel destroyed by unfaithfulness
   to Yahweh

The historical reality 69

Israel and Judah 70

The prophets 71

Elijah 72

Normal worship in the divided kingdoms 75

Festivals and history 76

Hebrew goddesses 79

The feminine face of the divine 80

Asherah 81

Anat 82

7. By the Waters of Babylon 84

The official version: a repentant return to the true faith

The political reality 85

Monotheism or capitulation 86

The great flood 88

The Epic of Gilgamesh

Noah 89

Similarities and differences 90

The creation 92

Marduk and Tiamat

The chaos monster in the Old Testament 94

Adam and Eden 95

The Genesis 1 creation account 96

Key points of the account 97

Babylonian elements in the account 99

8. Polytheism and Monotheism 102

The advantages of polytheism 103

Explanatory power

Emotional satisfaction 105

Grounding in nature 106

Scope for creative action 107

Realism about humanity 108

Re-evaluating the pagan roots 109

Notes 111

Further Reading 124

Bibliography 126

With thanks to Tricia:

"Till a' the seas gang dry, my dear,
And the rocks melt wi' the sun ..."

PREFACE

I have written this book primarily for two sorts of reader, both of whom love the adventure of thinking about religion and neither of whom is an academic specialist.

The first is a non-Christian, non-Jewish and possibly non-religious person who is currently exploring spirituality in the pagan or New Age areas. This reader is offered an opportunity to cast a radical but sympathetic eye over one of the key sets of sacred writings of the ancient world, and to find many traces of the old pagan gods hiding in unexpected places within its pages.

The second is a modern Christian or Jew, but one who is dissatisfied with conservative and fundamentalist readings of the Bible or Tanakh. This reader is offered an approach based upon Old Testament studies as it has developed in western universities over the last 130 years. It does not assume that the sacred writings are "right", and does not try to show that they are consistent with modern versions of monotheistic faith. But then neither is the approach hostile. It traces the evolution of religious ideas in the period from 1500 to 500 BCE in a way which I hope will be stimulating and challenging.

The book may also be of use to a third sort of reader, someone about to embark upon a course of study in Theology or Religious Studies and who is looking for a short, radical introduction to Old Testament religion. My hope is that such a reader will be excited by the content and encouraged to read further in more technical texts on the subject.

It is quite possible to read this entire book without ever opening a copy of the Old Testament. However most readers will want, at least at some point, to verify that the texts really do say what I claim they do. Such readers are spoiled for choice when it comes to English translations. All are essentially fine, but for those intending to buy one I suggest the New Revised Standard

Version (NRSV). This sticks close to the Hebrew text, uses inclusive language where possible, and is a popular choice of university Theology departments for these reasons. The English quotations from the Old Testament in this book are my own translations from the original Hebrew.

There are four sets of people I would like to thank. The first is Richard Coggins, previously of King's College London, who first introduced me to the study of the Old Testament with great wit, patience and good humor some thirty years ago. The second are the students of Westminster Under School in London, who had the good grace to be enthusiastic about the Old Testament when I taught it to them for six years. The third is Graham Harvey of the Open University who made several helpful suggestions.And the last are all the many anonymous writers and editors of the Old Testament, who labored long and hard to preserve for us all one of the great jewels of the world's religious heritage.

Philip West
www.philip-west.com
London 2011

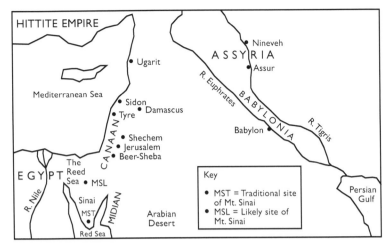

1. The Wider World of the Old Testament

2. Israel and Judah before the Exile

I

INTRODUCTION

The word of Yahweh came to Abram in a vision: "Fear not, Abram, I am your shield; your reward shall be very great ... Bring me a heifer ... a she-goat ... and a ram, three years old, a young bird and a turtledove." And Abram brought him all these, cut them in two, and laid each half separated from its other half ... and when the birds of prey swooped down on the carcasses, Abram drove them off.

Now as the sun set, an unnaturally deep sleep fell on Abram, and behold dread and great darkness came over him ... And when the sun had set and it was dark, behold, a smoking brazier and a flaming torch passing between the pieces ...[1]

This quotation is taken from the Christian Old Testament (the Jewish Tanakh), but it clearly has little to do with religion as currently practiced by either Christianity or Judaism. Instead it describes an essentially pagan religious experience and ceremony. Here is a ritual of covenant-making which, in a similar form, is well known among many ancient peoples. The partners to the covenant (the solemn treaty) walk through a lane between halved animals, invoking a curse upon themselves if they break their agreement with each other. Abram's god makes a covenant with him by appearing as a smoking fire pot and a flaming torch, and his appearance is accompanied by a feeling of intense supernatural dread.

This is far from the only point in the Old Testament where the hero of the story takes part in pagan practices. Repeatedly older sets of beliefs show through the veneer of monotheism which later editors have applied to their sources. The aim of this book is to extract the earlier paganism from its later monotheistic setting: to expose the originally pagan religion that underlies the sacred writings of Judaism and Christianity.

What is the Old Testament?

What Christians call the Old Testament is also the whole of the sacred texts (Tanakh) of Judaism. The content is the same in the two cases[2] but the order of the material is different, implying differences in how the two sets of compilers viewed it. Written mainly in Hebrew, the Old Testament makes up the first three quarters of the Christian Bible.

The Old Testament is not "a book" as such; it is much more like the library of an entire religious culture. Written down gradually over the course of maybe 800 years, it contains that culture's history, law, hymns and wisdom sayings, and the writings of its prophets.

The culture which produced it evolved considerably during the time of writing, and this is partly reflected in changes to the name of the people involved. Early on they are called the Hebrews (hence the name of the sacred language, "Hebrew"), then Israelites, and finally, from the sixth century BCE, Jews. They lived in a small section of hill country, not much bigger than Wales or New Jersey, located in the eastern Mediterranean. They shared many characteristics, including a language, with the other peoples of the region who are usually known as Canaanites.

The significance of the Old Testament

The Hebrew sacred texts were gradually written down from about 1000 BCE, when the Israelites first acquired a centralized administration and a literate class of scribes employed by the early kings David (about 1000 – 970 BCE) and Solomon (about 970 – 930 BCE). However they contain stories from much older times passed on, as was usual in the ancient world, by word of mouth.

Now we do have older western religious texts, particularly from Mesopotamia, Egypt and Syria, but these are fragmentary and nothing like as extensive or wide-ranging. So in reading the Old Testament we are reading some of the very earliest accounts of humanity's religious beliefs and practices. This bears repeating. Here we have many of the oldest western religious writings, and memories from the dawn of western civilization. The Old Testament is a prime source for the early pagan beliefs of humanity as a whole.

The extent, nature and survival of these texts is in fact quite remarkable. The group and area which produced them was small, rarely politically independent, and dwarfed by the empires of Egypt and Mesopotamia ranged on either side. Yet these writings have survived, and still nourish ongoing world religions, while the scriptures and religions of the larger empires have been largely lost and forgotten.

However for most modern western people the Old Testament is literally a closed book. Even among practicing Christians it has a reputation for obscurity, tedium and barbarity, with its god viewed as cruel and domineering or worse. Most non-Jews and non-Christians, including most pagans, simply assume that it has nothing useful to teach them.

This book aims to change that attitude by using the sacred Hebrew texts to expose the fascinating world of ancient Israelite religion, a religion much closer to polytheistic paganism than the official lines from Christianity and Judaism would have us believe. The book makes use of the best of Old Testament scholarship as practiced in western universities over the last 130 years. The findings of this scholarship are largely unknown to the average church or synagogue attendee, but they reveal a colorful kaleidoscope of ancient beliefs that is surprisingly attractive.

The official plot of the Old Testament

The Old Testament is not the work of a single author, but of many different people writing over the course of several centuries. The writings grew gradually, were collected and edited, and went through several revisions. They reached the form in which we now have them between about 500 and 200 BCE, and as such are the work of final editors working at that time.

Old Testament scholarship generally recognizes at least three earlier collector-editors involved in this process. The earliest, codenamed "J", worked round about the time of Solomon (tenth century BCE) and wove the traditional stories known to him into a coherent plot running from the creation of the world to the invasion and possession of the holy land of Israel/Canaan. The second, codenamed "D", worked around the seventh or sixth centuries BCE and interpreted the history of the Israelites since that invasion in terms of their faithfulness or otherwise to their god Yahweh. The viewpoint of "D" is similar to that of the Israelite prophets. The third, codenamed "P", worked around the sixth or fifth centuries BCE and reinterpreted the whole scheme from the viewpoint of the sacrificial priesthood. The final editors of the whole thing agreed in essentials with "P".

These editors have between them imposed an overall plot on the texts so that they fit together into a coherent whole. The plot concerns the history of the Israelite people and their dealings with their god, and goes like this:

- The one true God, a male deity called Yahweh[3], chooses Abraham[4] as his worshiper. Yahweh promises to make a great nation out of Abraham and gives him Canaan (roughly modern-day Israel) to live in.
- Abraham has a son called Isaac, whose son in turn is Jacob (also called Israel). Jacob fathers twelve sons and the whole family migrates to Egypt to escape a famine.

Eventually their descendants, the Israelites, are enslaved there.

- Moses is chosen by Yahweh to rescue his people from slavery. He leads them out of Egypt across the Red Sea, gives them the Ten Commandments at Mount Sinai, and takes them back across the desert to the promised land of Canaan. Yahweh forms a pact called the Covenant with the Israelites: provided they keep his commandments, and worship no other gods apart from himself, he will protect them and favor them as his special people.

- The Israelites capture Canaan under Joshua at the point of the sword, putting many of the inhabitants to death on Yahweh's instructions. They eventually form a great nation under the kingship of David, whose son Solomon builds the Temple in the capital Jerusalem.

- However the kings and the people continually break the Covenant, disobeying Yahweh's commandments and straying off to worship the Canaanite gods. Yahweh lambasts them for this through his mouthpiece the prophets, but to no avail. Eventually he loses patience, has Jerusalem and the Temple destroyed by the Babylonian armies, and the people are carried off into exile in Babylon.

- About forty years later Yahweh relents and a remnant of the exiles return to rebuild Jerusalem and the Temple. The Old Testament ends with the people (now called Jews) hoping for the restoration of greatness and independence under a new King David.

Implicit in this story are two editorial points of view which inform the whole of the Old Testament.

The first is a clear distinction between the Israelites on the one hand and their neighbors the Canaanites on the other, both in terms of descent and in terms of religion. The Israelites are believed to be a distinct people, who invaded Canaan from the outside bringing their own religion with them, and who struggled to displace the people who previously lived there. And the pagan religion of the Canaanites is believed to be thoroughly evil, quite different from the pure, ethical monotheism that is the true Israelite faith. There is no connection and can be no peace between the two communities, socially or religiously.

The second is the belief that all of the Israelites share direct descent from the founding fathers, Abraham and Jacob/Israel, who were the first to worship their god and founded their religion.

The reality underneath
So this is how the final editors of the Old Testament would like us to read the ancient texts. But it is possible to strip away their viewpoint and see what the old stories themselves originally said. For although the editors clearly felt free to add to the ancient stories they received, and to put them into a framework expressing their own beliefs, they generally did not just rewrite them from scratch. They left the stories more or less intact, even when they didn't fit the case they were trying to make.

If we separate out the ancient stories from the later viewpoint, and work with the stories alone, then almost every point of the "official plot" outlined above is shown to be a misrepresentation. Instead of a single God dealing consistently with a single people over hundreds of years, we find a great diversity of groups, beliefs and practices. Instead of a distinctive Israelite religion which is totally different from that of the Canaanites, we find a religion gradually emerging from a Canaanite source, sharing a past and a great many features with it. And instead of a consistent monotheism, what we find for much of Israelite history is a complex, polytheistic paganism.

A note on translations, footnotes and paganism
It is not necessary to look up any of the notes (indicated by small

numbers in the text like this[27]) while reading the book, but they are provided for three main reasons. Primarily they provide references to the passages from the Old Testament and other works quoted and summarized. Sometimes they follow up interesting sidelines that would otherwise interrupt the flow of the argument. And occasionally they refer to other books where complex issues are explained in more detail. The notes for each chapter are found at the end of the book.

The quotations from the Old Testament are my own translations from the original Hebrew. For those who want a copy of the Bible to read for themselves, I recommend the New Revised Standard Version (NRSV). This retains a lot of the poetry of the old King James Version of 1611 while updating its archaic language, correcting its mistakes, and using inclusive language where possible. It sticks close to the Hebrew text, which makes it a popular choice in university Theology departments. However any English translation of the Bible is fine provided you remain aware of its limitations. The Hebrew of the Old Testament is frequently ambiguous, so any translation takes decisions about the likely meaning of the text with which other translations may disagree.

The exact meaning of the term "paganism" is a contentious issue, particularly among modern pagans themselves. The British-based Pagan Federation defines it as including any polytheistic or pantheistic nature-worshiping religion,[5] while in the past the term was often used to denote any religion apart from the western monotheisms of Judaism, Christianity and Islam. In this book I use it in broadly the second sense: for all the beliefs and practices of the peoples surrounding the Israelites that were originally unconnected with their national god Yahweh. These beliefs and practices were frequently pagan in the first sense as well, as we shall see. My aim is to show how great was the influence of this paganism on the evolution of Israel's faith and on its sacred writings.

THE RELIGION OF THE PATRIARCHS

And the king of Sodom went out to meet Abram ... at the Valley of Shaweh. And Melchi-zedek, king of Shalem, brought out bread and wine. And he was a priest to *el elyon*. And he blessed him and said, "Blessed be Abram by *el elyon*, maker of heavens and earth; and blessed be *el elyon* who has given your enemies into your hand!" And he gave him a tenth of everything.[1]

The official version: Abraham the first worshiper of Yahweh
The editors of the Old Testament, the ones responsible for the "official plot" discussed in the last chapter, dealt with the earliest stage of Israelite religion in two significant ways:

- They joined up the old stories about Abraham, Isaac and Jacob, making these figures into sequential generations of a single family from which the whole Israelite nation was descended.
- They presented the names of the various gods worshiped by these ancestors as titles of the national god Yahweh.

In these two ways they claimed the ancient heroes of folk legend as the founders of both the nation and its religion.

According to the official plot, the one true God (Yahweh) chose Abraham, promised to make a great nation out of him, and gave him Canaan to live in. Abraham was miraculously given a son called Isaac to make this possible, and Isaac in turn had a son called Jacob or Israel (hence the name "Israelites"). Jacob then fathered twelve sons (Reuben, Simeon, Levi, Judah, Zebulun,

Issachar, Dan, Gad, Asher, Naphtali, Joseph and Benjamin) who were the ancestors of the twelve tribes of Israel. Preceded by Joseph, the family migrated to Egypt to escape a famine, at which point the story ends. All of these patriarchs are presented as worshiping the god Yahweh as their only god. Yahweh, who first revealed himself to Abraham, was God as worshiped by the Israelite nation and by the Jews after the exile.

Who were the patriarchs?

However Old Testament scholars are not happy with this version of events for three main reasons. Firstly the stories themselves, particularly the parts where the patriarchs[2] deal with their gods, do not fit well with the developed form of the religion represented by the later editors. Secondly many of the alleged titles of Yahweh are found rarely in the rest of the Old Testament and look suspiciously like the names of completely separate deities. And thirdly Abraham, Isaac and Jacob are shown as operating in different parts of the country,[3] as if they were originally the subjects of quite separate legends passed down by different sanctuaries or local groups. Because of all this, most Old Testament scholars regard the patriarchs in one of three ways.

Some see them as originally gods, who evolved into human heroes as the legends about them developed. However although this has happened often enough in the history of the world's religions, it does not seem to have happened here. The patriarchs in the stories do not display any divine attributes and seem to be thoroughly normal human beings.

Others view them as personifications of tribal groups. That is, when the story talks about the exploits of "Abraham", it is really talking about the exploits of a whole tribe. This is possibly the case, because in stories like the one above the patriarchs mysteriously turn into leaders of armies doing battle with neighboring tribes.

However most scholars regard the patriarchs as individual

but legendary human beings, whose stories were passed down at the sacred shrines they frequented. By molding them together in the official plot, the editors presented the disparate groups that eventually made up the Israelite nation as the descendants of a single biological family with a common and ancient religion.

Whichever of these is true, and in my opinion the third seems most likely, it is primarily with the gods worshiped by the patriarchs that we are concerned here.

The gods of the patriarchs

El

The word translated "god" or "God" in English versions of the Old Testament is the Hebrew word *el* (pronounced "ale"). This is significant for a number of reasons.

The Israelites developed in close contact with the Canaanite peoples, and El was the head god of the Canaanite pantheon. But in the Old Testament the word *el* has become generalized to mean a "god" in general. Thus Yahweh can be referred to as *yhwh el-ohe yisra-el*, "Yahweh the god of Israel". Notice in passing the *el* contained in the name "Isra-el": the Israelite nation is actually named after the Canaanite high god!

Now another level of complexity. When using the word "God" on its own to refer to Yahweh, the Old Testament generally uses the plural form *elohim*: "gods". It is not entirely clear why it does this. It may be similar to "the royal we" in dated British English, as in Queen Victoria's "We are not amused." If so, it is a way of giving Yahweh greater respect than the other gods in the region. Alternatively it may come from a period when Yahweh was believed to be president of a council of the gods, like those on Mount Olympus in Greece. Later the other gods were downgraded, leaving Yahweh in monotheistic isolation, but still referred to in the plural.

Either way, the use of the term *el* for the god of the Israelites suggests that Israelite religion developed out of Canaanite religion. This is in contrast to the view of the editors who believed that the two sets of gods, and the two religions, were completely and utterly separate.

The Canaanite high god

We used to know the Canaanite god El only from accounts contained in the Old Testament. But this changed dramatically in the mid-twentieth century following the discovery of a major Canaanite library at Ugarit in Syria. This library contains thousands of inscribed clay tablets dating from about 1400 BCE. Many of these are religious in content, containing accounts of El and the other gods of the Canaanite pantheon.

El is known here as the senior god of the Canaanites, the final authority in all human and divine affairs. His titles include "The Father of Men" ('ab 'adam)[4] and "The Kindly, The Merciful", echoing later descriptions of God in Christianity and Islam. He is also called "The Bull", signifying his strength as a warrior, and "The Creator of Created Things". The myths depict him sitting in royal estate in majesty and omnipotence, far beyond the menace of any evil power.

It seems likely that ideas about El were at least one source of Israelite conceptions of Yahweh as ruler, warrior and creator.

The gods of the fathers

Returning now to the Old Testament texts, each patriarch is shown there as having his own personal deity to whom he has sworn allegiance. The editors suggest that these gods were all in fact Yahweh, with each patriarch inheriting the worship of him from his father. But the different names given to these gods imply something different: that they were separate and unrelated deities in their own right. These personal deities are:

- *elohe abraham* (The God of Abraham)[5]

- *ahath yitsaac* (The Terror of Isaac)[6]
- *abir ya'acob* (The Mighty One of Jacob)[7]

There is also a fourth deity, *ro'eh eben yisrael* (The Shepherd, The Rock of Israel).[8] It is possible that Israel, whom the editors present as being Jacob under another name, was originally a fourth separate patriarch.

A significant characteristic of all these personal deities is their lack of attachment to any particular shrine. Instead they were attached to individuals, and could be worshiped equally well anywhere the individuals found themselves: a useful characteristic for the gods of semi-nomads like the patriarchs.

The gods of the local shrines

Alongside these personal gods, the patriarchs are also described as worshiping deities connected with local shrines. Once again the editors suggest that all these gods are manifestations of Yahweh, each name describing one of his divine characteristics. However in fact they were probably distinct and unconnected divinities. The list of these localized deities includes:

- *el elyon* (God Most High)[9] based at Salem (Jerusalem)
- *el rahi* (God of Seeing)[10]
- *el shaddai* (God Almighty)[11]
- *el olam* (God Everlasting)[12] based at Beer-sheba
- *el beth-el* (God of Bethel)[13] based, of course, at Bethel

Notice that each name contains the word *el*, reinforcing the point that these were Canaanite shrines dedicated to local Canaanite deities, not new shrines set up by the patriarchs themselves.

Conclusion

So overall we have the following picture of the patriarchs: three or four unrelated individuals, each with his own separate personal god, also worshiping local Canaanite deities at shrines. Not, as the editors suggest, sequential generations of the same family worshiping the same god: the national god Yahweh.

Individual stories of encounters with the divine

The Old Testament editors preserved several accounts of the patriarchs meeting with their gods, and these give us tantalizing glimpses into the religious beliefs and practices of the second millennium BCE. Because these accounts have virtually no point of contact with later versions of the faith, we can be pretty confident that the material is ancient rather than made up later on.

These stories mainly concern Abraham and Jacob, and we have met two of them already at the start of this chapter and Chapter 1. In the second Abraham is blessed by a priest of the Canaanite god *el elyon* and gives him the standard gift of a worshiper, a tenth of his wealth. In the first Abraham makes a solemn covenant with his god, *elohe abraham*, by undertaking a common pagan rite. Three more stories are described below.

Three divine figures by the Oaks of Mamre

Shortly after the events described above, Abraham has a divine revelation at his local Canaanite shrine, the Oaks of Mamre.[14] He is sitting at the door of his tent in the heat of the day when, on looking up, he sees three men standing there. After running to meet them and bowing to the ground, he instructs his wife Sarah to prepare a sumptuous meal for them as honored guests. One of the men (now identified as Yahweh) tells the childless Abraham, an old man with a wife past the menopause, that by next spring his wife Sarah will have a son. He then tells Abraham that he has decided to destroy the cities of Sodom and Gomorrah in the plain below because of their great wickedness. Abraham pleads with Yahweh that this will mean the destruction of many good people. He bargains Yahweh down to an agreement that if there are only

50, 45, 40, 30 and finally only 10 good people to be found in the cities that he will not carry out his threat.

As contained in the Old Testament this is a very strange passage indeed, but some of its awkwardness comes from the editor wanting to have Yahweh as the only god present. It is similar to other narratives, widespread in the ancient world, which tell of visits of divine beings to humans. In particular it resembles an ancient Greek story where the three gods Zeus, Poseidon and Hermes visit a childless man called Hurieus. After they have been served by Hurieus, the gods help him acquire a longed-for son, Orion, who comes to earth after ten months. Probably some such story underlies the Old Testament passage. The divine figures, appearing as ordinary men, are very different from the later editorial view of Yahweh as too powerful and remote to be seen by human eyes, or to be accompanied by any companions.

Jacob's ladder

In a famous passage set many years later, Jacob has a super-natural experience at what will become the major Canaanite shrine of *beth-el* ("House of El/God"). On a journey in a strange part of the country, he is forced to spend a night in the open. Taking one of the stones of the place as a pillow he lies down and sleeps:

> And he dreamed, and behold a staircase based on the earth and its head reached the heavens; and behold, messengers of God ascending and descending on it! (And behold Yahweh stood above it and said, "I am Yahweh, the god of Abraham your father ... behold, I am with you wherever you go.") ... And Jacob awoke from his sleep ... and he was afraid and said, "How fearsome is this place! This is as if it is a house of god; this is a gate of the heavens!" So Jacob arose in the morning, and he took the stone which he had put under his

head and set it up as a standing stone, and poured oil on top of it. He called the name of that place Bethel, but the name of the city was Luz at first.[15]

This is fairly clearly the foundation myth of the Canaanite shrine of Bethel. Shrines would often be established at places where people had significant religious experiences, and the site would be marked, as so often in western Europe, by erecting and sanctifying a standing stone.

It was a common view in the ancient world that there was a narrow place, like an umbilical cord, where intercourse between earth and heaven took place. Jacob realizes that he has stumbled upon it. The divine messengers are going back and forth between the earth and the upper divine world, not bearing prayers to the gods, but fulfilling the divine commands and supervising the earth. So this is *the* ultimate holy place: it is "a gate of the heavens" where the divine influence is channeled down and then out to the whole world. Hence the great importance of Bethel as a shrine in the early period covered by the Old Testament.

The editor, of course, wants to incorporate this story into the official Old Testament plot. He achieves this by adding the material I have placed in brackets: the god involved is said to be Yahweh, and the purpose of the vision becomes the revelation of Yahweh as the god of his father Abraham. This changes the whole thrust of the passage, but its older pagan meaning is still clearly visible through it.

Wrestling with a god

The last passage also concerns Jacob. It is set in the period just after he has tricked his brother Esau out of his birthright and is on his way back to see him for a difficult confrontation. Journeying through the countryside, he sends his family and flocks on across the River Jabbok as night is falling:

And Jacob was left alone and a man wrestled with him until break of day. When the man saw that he could not conquer Jacob, he reached for the hollow of his thigh; and Jacob's thigh was dislocated as he wrestled with him. And he said, "Let me go, for the day is breaking." But Jacob said, "I will not let you go, until you bless me." And he said to him, "What is your name?" And he said, "Jacob." Then the man said, "Your name shall no more be called Jacob, but Isra-el ("he who strives with God"), for you have striven with God and with men and have been victorious." Then Jacob asked him, "Tell me, I pray, your name." But he said, "Why do you ask my name?" And he blessed him there.

So Jacob called the name of the place Peni-el ("the face of God"), saying, "For I have seen God face to face, and yet my life is spared." And the sun rose upon him as he passed Penu-el, and he was limping because of his thigh.

Therefore to this day the sons of Israel do not eat the sinew of the hip which is upon the hollow of the thigh, because he reached for the hollow of Jacob's thigh on the sinew of the hip.[16]

The account as found in the Old Testament must have gone through several stages of reinterpretation. At its base is a story, common in the ancient world, of a man being attacked by a god, spirit or demon and managing to wrest something of its strength or a secret from it (the "blessing" in the narrative). It is common in such stories that the spiritual entity is only powerful during the night and must disappear at dawn. Also present is the ancient idea that to know the entity's name is to have power over it: by using its name it can be summoned in the future and compelled to do your bidding. The story was possibly the foundation myth of the shrine of Penu-el (also called Peni-el), accounting for its name.

The editors have appropriated this story for the official plot, replacing the demon with Yahweh and using it to link Israel with Jacob. Names were thought to capture the essence of the thing named. The name "Jacob" means "he supplants" and was linked to Jacob deceitfully tricking his elder brother Esau out of his rights of succession. Clearly such a character was not a particularly inspiring ancestor for the whole nation. So a divine change of the name to "Israel", meaning "he who strives with God", was appropriate and was justified by linking Jacob with the ancient tale.

Notice that the story also has other etiological elements (elements explaining unusual facts about the world). It gives reasons for a curious quirk of sacrificial practice (the attention given to the sciatic nerve during sacrificial slaughter) and possibly also for a form of cultic dance involving limping. A complex and multilayered text indeed, and one with a clear pagan background.

3

YAHWEH, MOUNT SINAI AND MOSES

On the third new moon after the Israelites had left the land of Egypt, on that day they came into the wilderness of Sinai ... On the third day in the morning there was thunder and lightning and a thick cloud upon the mountain ... so that all the people in the camp shuddered. And Moses brought the people out of the camp to meet God and they took their stand at the foot of the mountain. And Mount Sinai was wrapped in smoke over its whole face, because Yahweh descended upon it in fire; and the smoke of it went up like the smoke of a furnace, and the whole mountain shook violently ... Moses spoke, and God answered him in thunder.[1]

The official version: Yahweh as the only true God

The final editors of the Old Testament were monotheists. They were convinced that their god was the only true God, the sole creator of the universe, and that all other alleged gods were merely fictions. To these editors Yahweh *was* God with a capital "G", and the terms Yahweh and God were interchangeable. They also believed that Yahweh had been the sole Israelite god all along.

But in fact there is little reason to think that the patriarchs worshiped Yahweh at all: they worshiped a range of personal gods and the deities of the sanctuaries. And when Yahweh first appears, which is to Moses in the wilderness of the Sinai Peninsula, he appears not as God but as one tribal god among many.

Yahweh, Midian and Sinai

According to the stories preserved in the Book of Exodus,[2] Moses was an Israelite who was raised as an Egyptian in the royal palace. He had an Egyptian rather than an Israelite name,[3] which fits with this version of events. Fleeing from Egypt in young adulthood, he got a job working as a shepherd with the Midianites, a nomadic group located in the wilderness east of Egypt and south of Canaan. He married a Midianite woman and his father-in-law Jethro was the (or a) priest of the Midianite religion. The editors are unlikely to have made these details up, because elsewhere the Midianites are regarded as implacable enemies of the Israelites.[4]

It was while out in the wilderness tending the flocks of his father-in-law that Moses had his first experience of Yahweh. The passage is known as "the burning bush" episode:

> Now Moses was shepherd for his father-in-law Jethro, a priest of Midian. And he led his flock to the west side of the wilderness and came to Horeb, the mountain of God. And a messenger of Yahweh appeared to him in a flame of fire from the middle of a bush; and he looked and behold the bush was aflame, yet it was not being burnt up ... And God called to him from the middle of the bush, saying "Moses, Moses!" And he said, "Here am I." Then he said, "Do not come near; take off your shoes from your feet, for the place on which you are standing is holy ground" ... And Moses hid his face, for he was afraid to look at God ...
>
> Then God said to Moses, "I am who I am ... Thus you shall speak to the Israelites, 'I am has sent me to you.'"[5]

Note where this happens. The revelation occurs at "the mountain of God" or "Horeb". These are two alternative names regularly used for the holy mountain "Sinai" where later on Moses will receive the Ten Commandments.[6] Now the Midianites are thought to have worshiped their god at a local holy mountain. And Moses, living as a Midianite and working for one of their priests, is currently in their sacred area. An intriguing possibility follows: that Moses here has an experience of the Midianite god, and that Yahweh was originally a Midianite[7] tribal mountain deity, based in the wilderness to the south of Canaan.[8]

This possibility is consistent with another story, set after Moses has freed his people from Egypt. Moses is camped at "the mountain of God" when Jethro arrives:

> Moses went out to meet his father-in-law and bowed low and kissed him ... Then Moses related to his father-in-law all that Yahweh had done to Pharaoh and to the Egyptians on account of Israel ... And Jethro said, "Blessed be Yahweh who has delivered you from the power of the Egyptians and from the hand of Pharaoh. Now I know that great is Yahweh out of all the gods" ... And Jethro, Moses' father-in-law, offered a burnt offering and sacrifices to God.[9]

Now this story can be read in two different ways. The editors (who will have added the term "God" at the end) see it as describing Jethro's conversion to Yahweh which is sealed with a sacrifice. But it could equally be that Jethro already worships Yahweh. Realizing now that his own god is stronger even than the gods of the mighty Egyptians, he makes a sacrifice out of gratitude. The second reading probably captures the original thrust of the story and it supports the theory that Yahweh is a Midianite god.

Yahweh's home

That Yahweh was believed to have his home on Mount Sinai, in the wilderness to the south of Canaan, is also shown by scattered allusions elsewhere in the Old Testament. The oldest, written in archaic Hebrew and conceivably the most ancient Old Testament text of all, is The Song of Deborah in the Book of Judges.

The Song of Deborah

The Song of Deborah celebrates a notable victory of the Bronze Age Israelite tribes of the hill country against the better-armed Canaanites of the plains equipped with iron chariots. As a very ancient and stirring text, it is worth quoting at length:

> That the leaders led in Israel, that the people offered themselves willingly, bless Yahweh! ...
>
> In the days of Shamgar, son of Anath ... caravans ceased and those who went on journeys used the backroads. Champions were lacking, in Israel they were lacking, until you arose, Deborah, arose as a mother in Israel ... You riders on tawny asses, you who sit on saddle-cloths, you who walk by the way, tell it forth! To the sound of music at the watering places, let the glorious achievements of Yahweh be sung, the triumphs of his heroes in Israel! ...
>
> Yahweh, in your setting out from Se'ir, when you marched from the region of Edom, the earth shuddered, the heavens quaked, the clouds streamed down water. The mountains trembled before the face of Yahweh, yon Sinai before the face of Yahweh, the god of Israel.
>
> Then down to the gates marched the people of Yahweh. Up, up, Deborah! Up, up, utter a song! ... Then down marched the remnant with its chieftains; the people of Yahweh marched down for him against the mighty ...
>
> Then came the kings and fought, then fought the kings of Canaan. At Taanach, by the waters of Megiddo, they took no spoils of silver. From the heavens fought the stars, from their courses they fought against Sisera. The torrent of Kishon swept them away, the torrent attacked them, the torrent Kishon. March on, my soul, with might! ...
>
> So perish all your enemies, Yahweh! But your friends be

like the sun rising in his strength![10]

At the time of the battle in the second millennium BCE, their territory split into two halves by the Canaanite-occupied plain of Jezreel, the Israelites were in dire straits. Then under the leadership of Deborah they dared to do battle on the plains. The fight was accompanied by an exceptionally heavy rainstorm which bogged down the Canaanite chariots, giving a crucial advantage to the lightly armed Israelites. Yahweh, as a storm god, was responsible for the rain and thus gave them the victory.

Notice where Yahweh is described as coming from. Se'ir, Edom and Sinai are stylistic variations for the site in the wilderness where Moses had his revelation. Yahweh is seen as living there on his holy mountain and marching forth to do battle, recruiting the stars and the storm clouds of heaven to do his bidding.

Elijah at Horeb

Yahweh is still regarded as based on Mount Sinai in a story about the prophet Elijah dating from the ninth century BCE. Here, pursued by the agents of Queen Jezebel for having slaughtered her prophets, Elijah flees for his life to the sanctuary of Yahweh's stronghold:

> Then Jezebel sent a messenger to Elijah saying, "Thus may the gods do to me, and even worse, if by this time tomorrow I do not make your life as the life of one of them." Then he was afraid and he rose up and went for his life and came to Beer-sheba ... And he rose up and ate and drank and journeyed in the strength of that food forty days and forty nights to Horeb, the mountain of God. And he came there to a cave and lodged there.
>
> And behold the word of Yahweh saying to him ... "Go out and stand on the mountain before the face of Yahweh." And

behold Yahweh passes across, and a great and strong wind tears apart the mountains, and breaks the crags before the face of Yahweh, but Yahweh is not in the wind. And after the wind a shaking, but Yahweh is not in the shaking. And after the shaking a fire, but Yahweh is not in the fire. And after the fire the sound of a crushed silence. And when Elijah heard it he wrapped up his face in his cloak and went out and took his stand at the mouth of the cave. And behold unto him a voice, saying ... "Go, return on your way ..."[11]

Beer-sheba, the old cultic center of the patriarch Isaac, was in the extreme south of the country. By journeying further on from there Elijah was heading into the wilderness. Horeb, as mentioned before, is another name for Sinai. So Elijah sought sanctuary on the very holy mountain on which Yahweh had revealed himself to Moses and on which the Ten Commandments had been given. This was still Yahweh's true home. Here he remained unchallenged, unlike in the agricultural land to the north where the Israelites now lived.

Yahweh: a distinctive god

A particular problem often felt by Christians when reading the Old Testament is the need to equate the Yahweh of those texts with the God of Christianity. The Christian God generally takes one of three forms, or a mixture of them:

- A God of love and forgiveness, who even loves and forgives his enemies and instructs his worshipers to do likewise.
- The God of the philosophers, who is calm, impassive and above all human emotion.
- The ultimate embodiment of goodness, wisdom and power, however these are conceived.

None of these fits at all well with Yahweh, who is neither all-loving, nor calm, nor perfect.

The solution is to see Yahweh for who he is, a tribal deity of the Ancient Near East, rather than equating him with "God" in any of the senses above. If we do this we are freed up to investigate and appreciate Yahweh's character in the same way that we might appreciate Athena or Mercury, Odin or Isis. We are not committed to finding him perfect, and we can instead find him interestingly distinctive.

If this is done, the god who emerges has the following characteristics:

- Unlike most ancient deities he does not head or belong to a pantheon, or have a consort or children. He stands alone.
- He is male.
- He does not tolerate his worshipers also consorting with other gods. He regards this as unfaithfulness, an act of betrayal.
- He is human in form, rather than resembling an animal, plant or heavenly body. This is later expressed obliquely by the statement that human beings are made in his image or likeness.[12]
- He is a desert god, revealed in occasional powerful events like storms, earthquakes and volcanic eruptions. He is not associated with agriculture or connected with the annual cycle of vegetation.
- He performs selective nature miracles to help his followers, but does not consider it his role to intervene consistently in the world to eliminate human and animal suffering in general.
- He is passionate and given to violent outbursts of temper, rather than calm and impassive.
- He is a fearsome battle-god, fighting from heaven on behalf of his faithful worshipers.

- He is partisan. He defends his worshipers (provided they remain faithful) but shows no particular interest in the welfare of other human beings, often demanding their destruction.

This most emphatically is not the God of Christianity, in any of its three variants. Nor indeed is it the God of Judaism or Islam. It is much closer to the pagan gods of Greece and northern Europe, although for a pagan god Yahweh's insistence on exclusiveness is certainly unusual.

Many of these features of Yahweh are on display in the other events of Moses' life as presented in the second, third and fourth books of the Old Testament (Exodus, Leviticus and Numbers). The account is divided chronologically into five sections:

- the preparation of Moses for his mission[13]
- the plagues, Passover and escape from Egypt by crossing the Red Sea[14]
- the initial events in the wilderness[15]
- the making of the Covenant and the giving of the Law on Mount Sinai[16]
- the wilderness wanderings for forty years[17]

I will not attempt to summarize the whole of this material, which is long and often repetitive. Instead I will pick out a few stories which illustrate two themes. The first is Yahweh's distinctive nature, as outlined above. The second is the frequent use of magic by Moses, the greatest of all the leaders of the Israelites.

Magic in the Moses traditions

The difference between "religion" and "magic" is disputed, but a common way of distinguishing between them is this:

- Religion means communing with the divine, worshiping it

and asking it for help. The divine is in charge and its will is to be obeyed.

- Magic means manipulating supernatural powers for one's own ends. The individual is in charge and his or her will is paramount.

The two concepts often overlap in practice. For example the Roman Catholic Mass is clearly a religious ritual, but it is sometimes used magically to achieve a desired end. Perhaps it is best to see religion and magic as two ends of a continuum with many intermediate points. Nevertheless the distinction between the extremes is a useful one to bear in mind.[18]

The editors of the Old Testament were implacably hostile to magic in the above sense. Human beings should *obey* Yahweh, they believed; they should not attempt to *manipulate* him. Even to seek help from supernatural forces that are separate from him was considered impious. Yahweh is all-powerful and all-sufficient, and help should be sought from him alone.

Nevertheless, elements of magic can be seen in several of the Moses stories. So magic was clearly a significant component of ancient Israelite belief and practice. Several of the magical stories concern Moses' rod, or staff.

Moses' rod

The Egypt in which Moses grew up had developed magical theory and practice more fully than any other civilization of the ancient world. The Egyptians of the time believed that the universe was animated and controlled by a morally neutral spiritual power called *heka*. This could be manipulated magically by humans for their own ends as well as being used by the gods. They believed that this power could be invoked into material objects like statues to animate them. And their magical practices included the use of consecrated working tools, particularly staffs and wands.[19] In the light of this, consider the following passage which comes from the preparation of Moses for his mission:

> Yahweh said to him, "What is that in your hand?" and he replied, "A rod." And he said, "Cast it on the ground." And he cast it on the ground and it became a snake; and Moses fled away from it. But Yahweh said to Moses, "Put out your hand and take it by its tail." So he put out his hand and caught it, and it became a rod in his hand ...
>
> And Moses took his wife and his sons and set them on the ass, and went back to the land of Egypt; and Moses took the rod of God in his hand.[20]

Interestingly, the Hebrew word translated "snake" here has identical consonants to the word meaning "bewitchment", and the original Hebrew text was written without vowels. So the text hints that Moses is frightened here by the bewitchment, not just by a natural fear of snakes. The Hebrew word translated "serpent" in a later quotation is different and does not carry this connotation.

Moses' rod henceforth operates as a consecrated magical tool, in a similar way to the rods of the Egyptian magicians. This parallel is made particularly clear in the contest that follows in Pharaoh's court (on this occasion the rod being wielded by Moses' brother Aaron on his behalf):

> So Moses and Aaron went to Pharaoh and did as Yahweh commanded. Aaron cast his rod in the presence of Pharaoh and his servants, and it became a serpent. Then Pharaoh too called the wise men and the sorcerers; and they also, the soothsayer-priests of Egypt, did thus with their secret arts. For every man cast his rod, and they became serpents. But Aaron's rod swallowed their rods.[21]

Subsequently the rod is used to turn the water of the River Nile into blood as one of the plagues,[22] to divide the waters of the Red Sea so that the fleeing Israelites can escape from the pursuing Egyptian chariots,[23] and to cause a spring of water to gush from a rock in the wilderness when the people are dying of thirst.[24] The rod behaves for all the world like a wand imbued with inherent magical powers, rather than like a simple walking stick.

Battle with the Amalekites

Another use of magical power by Moses, again involving the rod, occurs shortly after the escape from Egypt into the wilderness. When the Israelites are attacked by an armed band of Amalekites:

> Moses said to Joshua ... "I will stand on the top of the hill with the rod of God in my hand." So Joshua ... fought with Amalek, and Moses, Aaron and Hur were on the top of the hill. And it happened that whenever Moses held up his hand Israel excelled, and whenever he lowered his hand Amalek excelled.
>
> But Moses' hands grew tired. So they took a stone and put it under him and he sat upon it. And Aaron and Hur held up his hands, one on one side and one on the other, so his hands were steady until the going down of the sun. And Joshua defeated Amalek and his people with the edge of the sword.[25]

As one Old Testament commentator notes: "In the story, the lifting up of the hands appears to have a strikingly impersonal magical effect. Yahweh is not mentioned at all in the whole section ... not even as having given Moses instructions for his action. A mysterious power seems to come from Moses which is focussed in the direction of the Israelite force, visible from the hill and thus reachable in a straight line by the beam of power."[26] It seems remarkably as if the Israelites are here given victory by a magical power wielded by Moses, rather than by Yahweh as such.

The bronze serpent

A third apparent use of magic occurs later in Moses' life, during the wilderness wanderings. As a punishment for the continual moaning of the Israelites about their lot:

> Yahweh sent fiery snakes among the people, and they bit the people so that many of the Israelites died. And the people came to Moses and said, "We have sinned ... pray to Yahweh that he take away the snakes from us." So Moses prayed on behalf of the people. And Yahweh said to Moses, "Make a bronze serpent and set it on a signal pole; and any who is bitten and sees it shall live." So Moses made a bronze serpent and set it on a signal pole. And if a serpent bit any man he would look at the bronze serpent and live.[27]

This story is interesting in two respects. Firstly it reflects an ancient magical belief that the power of dangerous creatures can be annulled by making images of them and performing ceremonies in the sight of the image.[28] Secondly, much later during the time of the monarchy, this same bronze serpent is found housed in the Jerusalem Temple with people making sacrifices to it. It has even been given a name: Nehushtan. With the evident approval of the editors, the pious king Hezekiah has it destroyed.[29] But this only serves to highlight the belief in its magical efficacy that was widespread up to that point.

Incidentally, we have evidence that this Old Testament story was considered highly significant in later periods. The author of John's Gospel in the New Testament uses it to explain how the Crucifixion brings salvation. Jesus, lifted up on a cross as the bronze serpent had been lifted up on a pole in the desert, saves men and women from death if they gaze upon this spectacle with the eye of faith.[30]

The circumcision of Moses' son

The last instance is a very obscure story, set when Moses is journeying with his wife Zipporah and his son(s) to confront Pharaoh after his call in the desert. Despite the fact that he is following Yahweh's explicit instructions:

> at a lodging place on the way Yahweh met him and sought to kill him. Then Zipporah took a flint knife and cut off her son's foreskin, and touched his feet with it and said, "Truly you are a bridegroom of blood to me!" So he let him alone ...[31]

The story makes little sense as it is written, so it presumably refers to an ancient practice unconnected with the plot.

Commentators speculate that circumcision was originally a magical ceremony carried out on a man on his wedding night. It was designed to ward off the threat of nocturnal attack by evil at this significant and vulnerable time. The wife cut off the man's foreskin with a flint knife (old flint being a more sacred material than newer metal) and touched his feet with the blood to confer protection. Later on the ceremony was changed into the consecration of a male child to Yahweh directly after birth. The editors operated with this newer meaning (hence Moses' son is circumcised), but they left in place parts of the older ritual which make no sense in the current context.

We can therefore suppose that the original story told of a demonic attack on Moses at a solitary and mysterious place in the desert, possibly on his wedding night. The editors replaced the malevolent demon with Yahweh, because they believed that he alone has the power of life and death over human beings.[32]

The escape from Egypt

The cluster of stories relating the escape of the Israelites from Egypt under Moses' leadership provides one more instance of a belief in magic and a good illustration of the distinctive nature of

Yahweh as a god. Found in Exodus chapters 5 – 15, it covers the plagues inflicted on the Egyptians, the Passover night, the flight of the Israelites, and their deliverance at the Red Sea. Of these, the Passover night and the deliverance at the Red Sea are the most important.

The Passover night
On returning to Egypt, Moses obtains an audience with Pharaoh and asks him to release his Israelite slaves. Not surprisingly Pharaoh is unwilling to lose his workforce just because he is asked by the spokesman of an unknown foreign deity. Moses' magic also fails to impress Pharaoh, because his own magicians are able to perform similar wonders (see the quotation above).

So Yahweh imposes a set of supernatural afflictions upon the Egyptians to convince them that it would be better to let his people go. These are the famous "plagues", starting with all of the fresh water in the country being turned to blood and concluding with the land being plunged into darkness for three full days. Finally, when all these have been unsuccessful:

Moses called all of the elders of Israel and said to them, "Take lambs for yourselves ... and kill the Passover lamb. Take a bunch of hyssop and dip it in the blood ... and touch, with the blood in the basin, the lintel and the two doorposts. And not a man of you shall go out of the door of his house until the morning. For Yahweh will pass through to slay the Egyptians; and when he sees the blood on the lintel and the two doorposts Yahweh will pass over the door, and will not allow the Destroyer to come into your houses to kill you" ...

And in the middle of the night Yahweh struck down all the firstborn in the land of Egypt, from the firstborn of Pharaoh who sits upon his throne down to the firstborn of the prisoner who was in the dungeon, and all the firstborn of the cattle. And Pharaoh rose up in the night, he and all his servants and all the Egyptians. And there was a great cry in Egypt, for there was not a house in which there was not one dead.

And Pharaoh called Moses and Aaron by night and said, "Rise up, go forth from among my people, both you and the Israelites ... Be gone and bless me also!"[33]

"The Destroyer" in the above passage appears without any explanation. It seems to be a demonic force that must be warded off magically using the blood of a sacrificial lamb. The blood is daubed upon the doors, the weak points of a house, to ward off the evil which could otherwise enter through them.

Many scholars speculate that Passover (Hebrew *pesah*) was originally an annual spring sacrifice undertaken by pastoral peoples herding their flocks on the steppes. Its occasion was the leaving of the winter grazing grounds in spring for the summer pastures. The beginning of these travels was a dangerous time for man and beast, especially for the newborn (of which the firstborn was the most precious). So an animal sacrifice was performed to ward off the evil powers that might otherwise attack with fatal consequences, especially, of course, at night. The editors transposed this sacrifice to the story of the flight from Egypt, and left in place some of its magical elements.[34]

Deliverance at the Red Sea

Having fled from Egypt, the escaping Israelites found their way to the safety of the wilderness barred by a stretch of water called in Hebrew the *yam suf*. This was mistranslated as "Red Sea" by the earliest Greek translation of the Old Testament, the Septuagint,[35] a mistake which has stuck ever since. Its proper translation is "Reed Sea", which refers to an area of reedy marsh and salt lakes between the northern end of the Red Sea and the Mediterranean. According to the earliest account of the story recorded by J:

When the king of Egypt was told that the people had fled ... he made ready his chariot and took his army with him ... And the Israelites lifted up their eyes and behold, the Egyptians were marching on after them and they feared greatly. And the Israelites cried out to Yahweh ... But Moses said to the people, "Do not fear, stand firm, and see the salvation of Yahweh which he will do for you today ... Yahweh will fight for you; you keep still" ... Then Moses stretched out his hand over the sea, and Yahweh drove back the sea by a strong east wind all night, and made the sea dry land, and the waters were divided. And the Israelites went into the midst of the sea on dry ground ... But Moses stretched forth his hand over the sea and the sea returned to its usual place when the morning appeared. And the Egyptians are fleeing as it advanced, and Yahweh shakes off the Egyptians in the midst of the sea ... Thus Yahweh saved Israel that day from the hand of the Egyptians, and Israel saw the Egyptians dead upon the seashore.[36]

The waters in this region, today as then, are variable in extent depending upon the winds and tides. The miracle consisted in the sending of a favorable wind in the night which created a dry route for the Israelites to cross under cover of darkness. This wind ceased at dawn, bogging down and trapping the heavy Egyptian chariots in the deepening water. This is similar to the event underlying the victory of Deborah as described earlier in this chapter. Again it depended upon Yahweh as a partisan, warrior, storm god being in charge of the weather. But notice here Moses performing a magical action with his arm that brings the elements, Yahweh's servants, to the aid of the Israelites.

One of the later editors, P, embellished the story by having two walls of water heaped up on either side of the crossing Israelites and then crashing back in upon the Egyptians. Although this is the version beloved of children's books and

Hollywood blockbusters, it is not the earliest version underlying the text.

The Covenant at Sinai

According to the Book of Exodus, three months after the Israelites escaped from Egypt they arrived back at Mount Sinai. The story is quoted at the start of this chapter and it continues as follows:

> And Yahweh came down upon Mount Sinai, to the top of the mountain. And Yahweh called Moses to the top of the mountain, and Moses went up. And Yahweh said to Moses, "Go down, warn the people, lest they break through to Yahweh to see and many of them fall" ...
>
> Now when all the people saw the thunder and the lightning and the voice of the trumpet and the mountain smoking, the people were afraid and shuddered and they stood far off. And they said to Moses, "You speak to us and we will listen; but let not God speak to us lest we die."[37]

Here we have Yahweh characteristically revealed in the violent events of storm, earthquake and volcanic eruption, rather than in the regular phenomena of sun, moon and seasons, as tended to be the case for the Canaanite gods. These phenomena suit his character well: a fierce, passionate deity with a power like the lightning that destroys instantly any who come too close to it.

Now it is pretty clear that the traditions have got jumbled up at this point. If you read Exodus chapters 19 – 34 you find Moses going up and down Mount Sinai like a yo-yo, often apparently forgetting whether he is supposed to be up or down. We also have large sections of detailed legislation, only conceivably relevant to the people once settled in the land of Canaan, inter-rupting the action. And in fact the whole account of the episode at Sinai (a massive section running from Exodus 19, through

Leviticus to Numbers 9) seems to have been dropped artificially into the account of the wilderness wanderings, which it interrupts. Many scholars therefore think that the placement of the Sinai events after the escape from Egypt is an editorial device, and that these stories were originally separate.

Be that as it may, some of the account of what happened at Sinai is very old, and it reveals ancient views about the characteristic nature of Yahweh. Partly this is seen in the events surrounding his appearance on the top of the mountain (already mentioned). Partly it is seen in the centerpiece of the whole story: the giving of the Ten Commandments.

The Ten Commandments
According to the texts as we now have them, at Mount Sinai a covenant is established between Yahweh on the one hand and the Israelites on the other. A covenant is a pact, deal or treaty, where both sides swear loyalty to each other and make promises as to their behavior in the future. In this case Yahweh promises to take the Israelites as his special holy people and to protect them by fighting on their side in wars. The Israelites in return must keep Yahweh's laws, the most important of which are summarized as the Ten Commandments.

Some of the Commandments were expanded with details and/or explanations later on. But in their original short form they probably read something like this:

1. You shall have no other gods alongside me.
2. You shall not make statues of any being in heaven or earth.
3. You shall not use my name for evil purposes.
4. You shall keep the Sabbath as a holy day and do no work during it.
5. You shall honor your father and mother.
6. You shall not murder.

7. You shall not commit adultery.
8. You shall not steal.
9. You shall not lie about your neighbor (in court).
10. You shall not seek to possess any of your neighbor's property.[38]

The last six of these laws are unremarkable: they are many of the rules which govern relationships between people in almost all societies. But the first four, concerning how the people should behave towards Yahweh, are unusual. Unfortunately the reasons behind the fourth Commandment (the Sabbath) are lost in the mists of time. But there are things to say about the other three.

The first Commandment is translated variously in different English versions of the Bible, but the Hebrew literally means "There will not be to you other gods before my face." Now "before my face" is Hebrew idiom for "in my presence". So Yahweh is demanding that he alone be worshiped, that the Israelites may not also worship other gods as an insurance offer. This highlights the unusual exclusiveness of Yahweh that we noted earlier in the chapter. Notice also that Yahweh does not *deny the existence* of other deities; it is just that they should not be *worshiped*.

In its later expanded form the second Commandment forbids making statues and then worshiping them, which implies a ban on worshiping idols as gods. However this just repeats the first Commandment which has already forbidden worshiping anything except Yahweh. So originally the Commandment probably ruled out making models of anything that might be used *in the worship of Yahweh himself*. This includes the "golden calf" which the people make while Moses is absent up Mount Sinai (see below). Underlying the Commandment is the ancient belief that an image captures the essence of the thing portrayed. By making an image of something used in worship, the worshiper might gain power over it, and thereby gain some magical power over Yahweh himself. This is not permitted. Yahweh is to remain in complete control. His power over the worshiper must not be compromised by attempts at magical manipulation.

The third Commandment is often translated "You shall not take the name of the LORD your God in vain", and then interpreted as meaning a ban on its use in swearing. However the Hebrew term translated "in vain", *lashaw'*, means either "worthlessly" or "deceitfully with evil intent". Behind the Commandment lies the idea that a person or deity is mysteriously present in their name. To use Yahweh's name carelessly is therefore to show a stunning lack of respect for the deity. But more than this: because the name has real power it can be used for evil purposes, for effective cursing. So the Commandment essentially bans the use of Yahweh's name in black magic.[39]

Notice, then, that two of the first three Commandments were originally directed against magical practices, on the basis that all power should reside with Yahweh alone. But of course laws are only promulgated against crimes that people are likely to commit. Which suggests that there was a great deal of magic, of both a positive and a negative kind, being practiced in ancient Israelite religion.

The golden calf
According to the Book of Exodus, while Moses was away on one of his extended visits to the top of Mount Sinai communing with Yahweh, the following happened:

> The people assembled in front of Aaron and said to him, "Up, make for us gods who will go before us. As for this Moses ... we do not know what has become of him" ... So all the people took off the rings of gold which were in their ears and brought them to Aaron. And he received it from their hands, and formed it with a stylus, and made a cast of a calf. And they

said, "These are your gods, Israel, who brought you up from the land of Egypt!" And Aaron saw this and he built an altar before its face.[40]

The passage implies that the people regarded the calf as a god, and proposed to follow this god rather than following Yahweh. But it is important not to take this at face value.

It seems probable that the story was projected back from a time several hundred years in the future when the Israelite kingdom split into two on Solomon's death (see Chapter 6). The king of the breakaway north, lacking access to the Jerusalem Temple, established two shrines for his people at Dan and Beer-sheba. In each of them he placed a large golden bull *as a symbol of Yahweh*, as was customary in all temples of the time. The south thoroughly disapproved of the breakaway north and its scorning of the Jerusalem Temple, and insulted the bulls by calling them "calves".[41] This condemnation was then projected back into the sacred prehistory of the Sinai desert to give it more clout, and was (deliberately?) misunderstood as a turning away from Yahweh to other gods.

So in this well-known story we are probably reading a piece of vitriolic polemic from another place and time, rather than a historical incident. But note, even so, the breach of the second Commandment. By making an image of Yahweh himself (as a bull) the king of the north sought to gain magical control over him. This must be rejected: Yahweh is to be obeyed, not controlled.

4

RELIGION IN CANAAN BEFORE
KING DAVID

And they carried the ark of God upon a new cart, and brought it out of the house of Abinadab which is on the sacred hill; and Uzzah and Ahio the sons of Abinadab were driving the new cart ... And David and all the house of Israel were dancing happily before Yahweh with abandon, with songs and harps and lutes and tambourines and castanets and cymbals. And when they came to the threshing floor of Nacon, Uzzah reached out to the ark of God and took hold of it, because the oxen stumbled. And Yahweh's nose glowed hot against Uzzah; and God struck him down there because he reached out to the ark; and he died there beside the ark of God.[1]

The official version: the revealed religion of Sinai

According to the Old Testament as we now have it, the contents of Israelite religion were revealed to Moses on Mount Sinai in the desert. Before the Israelites ever entered their promised land of Canaan their religion was complete in all its essentials, including its beliefs about God, laws and forms of worship.[2] When the Israelites invaded and occupied Canaan under the leadership of Joshua they did so as a unified people, replacing the Canaanites and their religion with something totally different. In the following centuries they repeatedly lapsed from their true religion by dabbling in Canaanite practices. However when they returned it was a return to the original form of their faith; there was no evolution, development or progression in their religious ideas.

This is the viewpoint of the later editors. It is found in the editorial sections of the Book of Joshua, telling of the invasion and conquest of Canaan, and in the editorial framework of the Book of Judges which covers the period between the conquest and the monarchy.

What actually happened

But the stories themselves show a different reality. They imply that Israelite religion was completed in Canaan itself, not in the desert; that the Israelites entered as many separate bands largely by peaceful migration, not as a unified nation by military conquest; that most of the Canaanites remained in place practicing their religion, rather than being eradicated by the newcomers; and that far from the Canaanite and Israelite religions being totally separate, later Israelite faith contained many Canaanite elements.

The main evidence against a unified armed conquest is the contradictory account found in the Book of Judges. According to the Book of Joshua, "Joshua defeated the whole land, the hill country and the Negeb and the lowland and the slopes, and all their kings; he left none remaining, but utterly destroyed all that breathed, as Yahweh the God of Israel commanded." The whole land was then divided up among the Israelite tribes.[3] However in the Book of Judges, in theory set immediately afterwards, the Canaanites are still very much alive and kicking and the Israelites possess only fragments of the hill country.[4] Hints in the Book of Joshua also suggest that only the central highlands were occupied, the "all Israel" view being a later editorial device.[5]

Most Old Testament scholars therefore think that the settlement of Canaan was gradual, patchy, uncoordinated and largely peaceful. They speculate that only one group of Israelites (sometimes called "The Moses Host") had escaped from Egypt and had adopted Yahweh at Sinai, with the other groups coming round to their way of thinking slowly, if at all. It is with the adventures of The Moses Host that the Book of Joshua is concerned, not with the adventures of all the Israelite tribes.[6]

Be that as it may, our main interest lies with the religion of the period. This involved interactions between the indigenous Canaanite cults, the Yahwistic religion of The Moses Host, and the religion of the other Israelites.

The evidence from Ugarit

The Canaanite religion that the incoming Israelite tribes encountered is now well known to us, thanks to a major archaeological find at Ugarit in Syria. Excavations from 1929 onwards uncovered the remains of a Canaanite city state which had flourished in the second half of the second millennium BCE. As mentioned in the Introduction, this gave us independent information about the god El. It also gave us much besides.

The finds at Ugarit include a large number of texts (often referred to as the Ras Shamra texts) written on clay tablets in cuneiform and Akkadian and dating from about 1400 BCE. The texts are lists of gods, sacrifices, ritual regulations and prayers, and some are longer poetic epics about the exploits of the gods.[7] The Ugarit finds confirm archaeological discoveries made elsewhere in Syria and Palestine, and fit with allusions to Canaanite religion in the Old Testament itself. All this encourages us to believe that Ugarit was representative of Canaanite religion as a whole.

The Canaanite gods

As already mentioned, the Canaanite gods were organized into a pantheon under the headship of the god El. The number of gods was large, and doubtless included many minor gods worshiped at local sanctuaries. But as shown in the Ugarit finds, the main high gods were as follows:

- **El** presided over the divine assembly as king. His dwelling place, where the other gods might seek him out if they needed counsel, was in the far distance where the waters above the heavens met those below the earth. His titles included "father of the gods", "father of humankind", "creator of all creatures", "creator of the earth", "king", "bull El", "the holy one", "the friendly one" and "El the one with feeling". Although rather more remote than some of the other gods, he had not been usurped by them as sometimes happened to the older ruling gods in other pantheons.

- **Baal** took center stage in the poetic myths. Described variously as the son of El or son of Dagon, he lived on Mount Zaphon to the north of Ugarit. His proper name was Hadad, and Baal was really a title meaning "lord", "owner" or "husband". He was the god of storms, rain and fertility, and his other titles included "mighty one", "ruler", "cloud-rider" and "prince of the earth".

- **Asherah** was the female consort of El, and with him was worshiped as the creator of the gods. She could intercede effectively with El on behalf of others (compare the role of the Blessed Virgin Mary in Roman Catholic Christianity).

- **Anat** was the sister and consort of Baal. Her nature was a lusty combination of exaggerated sexuality and blood-thirstiness: we hear of her in a murderous rage as she waded up to her waist in the blood of enemies, walking over human skulls while detached human hands fly around her like locusts. Astarte and Ashtoreth were probably alternative names for Anat.

- **Dagon**, an import from another pantheon, was a god of grain and a bestower of fertility. He had a temple next to Baal at Ugarit. He was the major god of the Philistines further to the south, with temples at Gaza and Ashdod.

The poetic myths

Although not the creator, Baal was the preserver of creation. He achieved this preservation through cycles of actions that were told in poetic myth and re-enacted annually in temple ritual. In the myths Baal is set the tasks of gaining a kingdom, securing it by building a temple, and defending it against his divine enemies. These enemies are **Yam**, prince of the sea who threatens human life by flooding, and **Mot** the god of death who personifies the summer drought with its withering of the vegetation.

In the most important drama, Baal descends to Mot's underworld in the early summer, taking the rain with him so that life dries up. This institutes the reign of Mot which lasts over the summer drought. El and Anat both mourn Baal's death, and El institutes Asherah's son Athtar as a replacement on her advice. Athtar proves to be incompetent (which may personify the drying up of rivers and springs), so Anat determines to act. She slays Mot, and Baal returns and drives off the incompetent Athtar. Baal is reinstated in his temple as king, peace and goodwill are re-established, and rain, life and fertility are restored.[8]

The Canaanite cult

There were two main types of center for Canaanite worship: the "high places" and the temples. The high places were not necessarily on the tops of hills, but all had a raised altar for sacrifices along with a grove of trees. Many had "Masseboth", standing stones shaped to represent deities, and a wooden pole or "Asherah" to represent the goddess of the same name. Many high places are recorded in the Old Testament as being scattered around the Israelite territory. Building an actual temple, thought of as a house for the deity, was an important part of the recognition given to a high god, but was much more expensive and therefore rarer. Those at Ugarit were equipped with altars, utensils for sacrifice or other worship, and images or symbols of the gods in stone, metal or ivory.

As regards male personnel, at Ugarit there was an organized priesthood headed by a high priest. Under him were twelve families of priests, then a lower tier of priestly assistants, then singers and craftsmen. Canaanite religion was in essence a fertility cult with a strong strain of sexuality, and this was facilitated by female cult prostitutes attached to the sanctuaries. Having ritual sex with them was thought to strengthen the deities and keep the powerful forces of life flowing and active.

Aside from ritual sex, the other regular activities at the sanctuaries included recitation and re-enactment of the myths, sacred dance, divination, prayer and the singing of hymns. But the key activity, as in almost all ancient religions, was "sacrifice". This was divided into three main types, the last two performed by a priest:

- Giving gifts of food and drink for the god to consume.
- (Whole) burnt offerings, where the whole of an animal was burned on an altar as a gift to the god.
- Sacrifice proper. The blood of a sacrificial animal was poured over the base of the altar, and the fat and intestines were burned as an offering to the god. The meat was cooked (often boiled) and was eaten by the worshipers as a sacred meal of communion to bind them closer to the deity. Here, it seems, is the original root of the Christian Eucharist or Mass.[9]

Israelite and Canaanite religion

When the Israelite tribes entered Canaan they found both a different way of life and a more sophisticated religion. Previously semi-nomads making a living from herding animals, they encountered settled towns and villages based on agriculture. And previously practicing quite a simple form of religion, they encountered the organized cult outlined above.

There was irresistible pressure to adopt at least some elements of the new religion, especially as it was adapted to the agricultural way of life which many now took up.

A lot of the Israelites seem to have taken over the Canaanite religion wholesale. But the Yahweh-worshipers, committed to an exclusive worship of their only god, were forced to seek a compromise. The main features of this, which determined the nature of Israelite religion for the next 500 years or so, were as follows.

El

El was simply assumed to be Yahweh under another name, which opened the way for an amalgamation of the two religions. It also led to a softening in beliefs about the character of their god. The dangerous, passionate and occasionally sinister features of Yahweh were softened by the prudence, wisdom, moderation, patience, forbearance, mercy and compassion for the weak of El. El's function as creator of the world was also added. This implies that many of the most attractive aspects of the God of later monotheism can be traced to a pagan source.

Several of the Psalms (hymns) in the Old Testament may originally have been Canaanite. In two cases at least, hymns to El were apparently adopted and applied to Yahweh instead:

> The heavens make known the glory of El, and the sky announces the work of his hands;
> Day by day they pour out speech, and night by night declare knowledge.
> There is no speech and there are no words, their voice is not heard;
> But into all the earth their voice goes forth, their words to the end of the world.
> In them he has pitched a tent for the sun,
> Who comes forth like a bridegroom leaving his canopy,

Rejoicing like a strong man to run his race.
From one end of the heavens is his rising, and his circuit to
    the end of them,
And there is nothing hidden from his heat.

Father of the fatherless and bringer of justice to widows
Is God in his holy dwelling-place.
God gives the abandoned his home;
He leads out the prisoners to prosperity.[10]

Baal

Some of the Yahweh-worshipers also equated Baal with Yahweh, while others rejected him as Yahweh's rival. The latter group became particularly powerful during the monarchy and eventually triumphed, but at this early stage they were less influential. The fact that *baal* can also be a common noun meaning "lord" no doubt helped the process of identification. It is notable that several early Israelite names are compounds containing Baal, for example Eshbaal, a son of King Saul.

"Lord" of course is a suitable way of addressing a male deity to whom you have sworn allegiance, including one like Yahweh. The modern Christian habit of addressing God or Christ as "Lord" may be traced back to this point, and originally indicated the pagan god Baal rather than Yahweh as such.

As with El, some features of Baal were transferred to Yahweh including the idea of him riding upon the clouds. And once again some of the Old Testament psalms were originally Canaanite and addressed to Baal; simple changes in the divine names made them suitable for Israelite worship. For example:

Sing of God, sing praises to his name;
Prepare a road for him who rides upon the clouds.
Yahweh/Baal is his name, exult before him.[11]

In the following psalm the ideas of the god being enthroned as king, the worship of the deity by other gods in a holy assembly, and the mentions of forests, waters and Lebanon seem to imply a Canaanite source rather than an Israelite wilderness setting. I have taken the liberty of translating the Hebrew *yhwh* as "the Lord" in the version below, which then works equally well as addressed to either Yahweh or Baal:

> Ascribe to the Lord, sons of gods;
> Ascribe to the Lord glory and strength.
> Ascribe to the Lord the glory of his name;
> Worship the Lord in the splendor of holiness.
> The voice of the Lord is upon the waters, the god of glory thunders,
> The Lord, upon many waters;
> The voice of the Lord in power, the voice of the Lord in majesty.
> The voice of the Lord breaks the cedars, the Lord shatters the cedars of Lebanon.
> He makes Lebanon skip like a calf, and Sirion like the son of a wild ox.
> The voice of the Lord flashes forth flames of fire;
> The voice of the Lord makes the desert dance,
> The Lord makes to dance the wilderness of Kadesh.
> The voice of the Lord twists the oaks, and strips the forests bare,
> And in his temple all cry "Glory!"
> The Lord sits enthroned over the heavenly ocean,
> The Lord sits as enthroned as king for ever.
> The Lord gives strength to his people.
> The Lord blesses his people with peace.[12]

The cult

When it came to worship, the incoming Israelites seem to have taken over the Canaanite practices pretty much lock, stock and barrel. The high places were adapted for the worship of their own gods including Yahweh, the sacrificial system with its three divisions was adopted unchanged, and a dedicated priesthood was established or continued. The local agricultural festivals were also celebrated. All these things are alluded to in stories scattered throughout the books of Judges and Samuel.

Some details of the life at an ancient Israelite sanctuary are given for Shiloh, a center which was specifically constructed for Yahweh worship in the central hill country. This was the location of Samuel, the most important religious leader in the period just before the start of the monarchy. Unusually, Shiloh was a temple, not just a high place. The local people used to go there for an annual sacrifice.[13] The temple was run by a hereditary priesthood, and parents might give a son to serve there as a gift to Yahweh, accompanied by gifts of a bull, flour and wine.[14] The priests would be given a share of the cooked meat from the sacrifices for their subsistence.[15] They would wear a linen ephod while serving in the sanctuary,[16] and could be consulted for oracles in return for a gift.[17] The annual sacrifice involved a communal meal prepared by a cook and blessed by the priest,[18] and the unmarried girls danced together afterwards in the adjacent vineyards.[19]

In a later period the Israelite cult, along with the Israelite laws, was traced back to a theoretical origin at Mount Sinai at the time of Moses. This gave it legitimacy and resulted in long sections describing arrangements for worship being inserted into the present books of Exodus, Leviticus, Numbers and Deuteronomy. But the truth of the matter? The later Israelite cult was essentially Canaanite, and therefore pagan.

For the rest of this chapter we shall examine three particular aspects of ancient Israelite religion as described in the old stories: divination, human sacrifice and the mysterious object known as "the ark".

Divination

There are several positive descriptions of divination in the early stories. Most involve two devices, both apparently taken over from Canaanite religion: the ephod, and the urim and thummim. Use of either to give or to seek guidance could be described positively as "consulting Yahweh".

The urim and thummim were sacred lots which gave "yes" or "no" answers to specific questions. For example, on one occasion when Saul was deciding whether he should go and fight the Philistines, he sought divine guidance but got no answer. Assuming this was because someone had sinned:

> Saul said to all Israel, "You shall be on one side, and I and Jonathan my son will be on the other side" ... And Saul said to Yahweh the god of Israel, "Why have you not answered your servant today? If this guilt is in me or in Jonathan my son ... give urim; but if this guilt is in your people Israel, give thummim." And Jonathan and Saul were taken, but the people escaped. Then Saul said, "Cast the lot between me and Jonathan my son." And Jonathan was taken. Then Saul said to Jonathan, "Tell me what you have done ... you shall surely die, Jonathan."[20]

The nature of the ephod is less clear, although it usually appears as an article of clothing.[21] Originally it had been the robe of the Canaanite goddess Anat as described in one of the Ugarit poems. Possibly this was then adapted as a cloak to put on the images of the gods in the sanctuaries. But in most of the Old Testament stories it is worn by a priest next to his heart, showing his ability to give oracles in the name of Yahweh. Giving oracular guidance seems to have been almost as important a part of a priest's role as performing sacrifices.

Apart from these two devices, there is one story where an oracle is sought using a medium. This occurs towards the end of

Saul's life when he seeks help from the medium of Endor:

> Now Samuel had died ... and Saul had got rid of the mediums and wizards from the land. The Philistines gathered and came and encamped at Shunem ... and Saul saw the army of the Philistines and he saw and his heart trembled greatly. And Saul inquired of Yahweh, but Yahweh did not answer him, either by dreams, or by urim, or by prophets. So Saul said to his servants, "Seek out for me a woman who is a lord of dead spirits that I may go to her and inquire of her" ...
>
> So they came to the woman by night. And Saul said urgently, "Divine for me a spirit ... bring up Samuel for me" ... And the woman saw Samuel and she cried out with a loud voice ... And the woman said to Saul, "I see a god coming up from the earth ... an old man is coming up and he is wrapped in a robe." And Saul knew that it was Samuel ... Then Samuel said to Saul, "Why have you disturbed me by bringing me up?" Saul answered, "I am in great distress ... I have called you to tell me what I should do" ... Samuel replied, "Why do you ask me, since Yahweh has turned from you and become your enemy? ... Yahweh has torn away the kingdom from your hand and given it to your neighbor David because you did not listen to the voice of Yahweh, and did not execute his fierce anger against Amalek ... Yahweh will give Israel with you into the hand of the Philistines, and tomorrow you and your sons will be with me" ... Then Saul fell at once full length upon the ground fearing greatly because of the words of Samuel ...[22]

Despite the later condemnations of mediums in the writings of the prophets, in this story there is no criticism of the use of an occult technique as such, and the technique is believed to work. The problem is not Saul's use of a medium; the problem is that he had previously been disobedient to Yahweh.

Human sacrifice

Human sacrifice was fairly common in the ancient world, especially in extreme circumstances. The practice was certainly banned later on in Israel, but there are two cases in the Old Testament where it is recorded without censure.

The first concerns the ambiguous character Jephthah, a one-time bandit who was recruited by the Israelites to fight off a threat from the neighboring Ammonites. Jephthah vowed that if Yahweh gave him victory over the Ammonites he would offer as a burnt offering whoever first came out of his house to meet him on his return home. Jephthah was victorious, then:

> Jephthah came to his house at Mizpah. And behold his daughter came out to meet him with tambourines and with dances, and she was his only child; besides her he had neither son nor daughter. And when he saw her he tore his clothes and said, "Alas, my daughter! You have brought me to my knees, such trouble you have brought upon me; for I have opened my mouth to Yahweh and I cannot take back my vow." And she said to him, "My father, if you have opened your mouth to Yahweh, do to me according to what has gone forth out of your mouth, seeing as Yahweh has avenged you on your enemies, on the Ammonites ... (But) let me alone two months, that I may walk and wander upon the mountains and weep on account of my virginity, I and my companions" ... And it came to pass that at the end of the two months she returned to her father and he did to her according to his vow which he had made.[23]

It is remarkable that Jephthah is not criticized for these actions in the text, even by the editors.

There is one more case where human sacrifice is demanded, and this is the famous case of Abraham's near-sacrifice of Isaac set in an earlier period. In this story Abraham's god demands that he sacrifice his only son Isaac as the ultimate test of loyalty, but spares Isaac once it is clear that Abraham is going through with it.[24] As with the Jephthah case, there is no hint of disapproval in the passage and Abraham, like Jephthah and his daughter, seems to accept that this is a normal part of the relationship between someone and their god. Which raises the possibility that human sacrifice was, indeed, an acceptable part of Israelite religion in the early days, as it was for example in neighboring Moab.[25]

The ark

The mysterious "ark" has captured the imagination of film-makers in recent decades, and it was clearly an important object in early Israelite religion (see the quotation at the start of this chapter). Allegedly constructed by Moses in the desert, it appeared at the invasion of Canaan under Joshua, was later located in the temple at Shiloh, was lost to the Philistines and then recovered, was brought to Jerusalem by David, and was finally placed in his newly built temple by Solomon. But what it looked like, and what its precise function was, are both unclear. Suggestions range from a box containing the Ten Commandments, images of the deity, or some other sacred object; to a throne on which Yahweh was thought invisibly to sit; to an emblem of a mutual defense treaty between the Israelite tribes.

The stories themselves portray the ark as possessing dangerous magical power of an essentially impersonal kind, not unlike that of high-voltage electricity. At the crossing of the River Jordan by Joshua, where it is carried by specially sanctified priests, the people are warned not to approach it closer than 2000 paces. Once the feet of the priests carrying it are in the water, the waters stop flowing and heap up upstream so the people can cross.[26] When captured and placed by the Philistines in the temple of their god Dagon, it topples the image of the god over and breaks off its head and hands.[27] It then makes the people of the city break out in tumors,[28] and kills seventy Israelites on its return because they dare to look inside.[29] When being transferred to Jerusalem, an attendant called Uzzah touches it to prevent it falling and is struck dead.[30]

More positively, the presence of the ark sometimes brings with it the effective protective presence of the divine. Its loss is regarded as a terrible tragedy and it is accorded ultimate respect. When the ark arrives in the Israelite camp during a war with the Philistines, the Israelites give a shout of triumph which strikes fear into the heart of their enemies.[31] When the priest Eli hears of its capture he falls backwards off his seat, breaks his neck and dies, and his daughter-in-law is catapulted into labor with the cry "The glory has departed from Israel, for the ark of God has been captured!"[32] And when King David brings the ark into Jerusalem he does so with sacred dances, wearing an ephod, and with sacrifices.[33]

Experts are divided. But one likely explanation for all this has the ark as an ancient, feared and respected magical object that was originally unconnected with Yahweh. Because it was so important, it was renamed the Ark of the Covenant and reinterpreted as a box made at Sinai to carry the tablets of the Ten Commandments.[34] Its dangerous and terrifying nature certainly connects well with some aspects of the Yahweh revealed at Sinai. But it was essentially another pagan element included in ancient Israelite religion, one less predictable and humane than the Canaanite high gods, and one which certainly did not sit easily with the religious views of the final editors.[35]

5

JERUSALEM, KING AND TEMPLE

He who sits in the heavens laughs; the Lord ridicules them.
Then he will speak to them in his anger,
And test them, terrifying them out of their senses:
"I have set my king on Zion my holy hill."
I proclaim the decree of Yahweh.
He said to me: "You are my son, this day have I begotten you.
Ask of me and I will make the nations your heritage,
And the ends of the earth your property."[1]

The official version: David the fulfillment of Yahweh's vision
According to the "official plot" of the Old Testament the reigns
of David and Solomon marked the high point in the fortunes of
Israel, religiously as well as in every other way. David was
chosen by Yahweh as the final culmination of his plans for his
chosen people. He established a divinely ordained dynasty that
was to rule the earth in righteousness as the agent of God
himself. Unfortunately the subsequent kings betrayed that
vocation, especially in the northern kingdom of Israel. But the
vocation itself was from Yahweh, and was to be reactivated in the
future by a "new King David" who would follow in the footsteps
of his illustrious forebear. The New Testament, in accord with
this view, also looked back to David as the greatest figure of the
Old Testament and was at pains to show that Jesus was
descended from him as the long-awaited Messiah.[2]

Now it is true that the reigns of David and Solomon marked
the high point in the existence of Israel politically. Under David
the Israelite tribes were united into an independent nation which
saw off the threats from the powers round about. Under his son

Solomon the nation even expanded into a small empire, annexing the surrounding non-Israelite states like Ammon and Moab. At no other stage in Israel's history was it ever a truly independent and united state.[3] But whether the reigns of these two kings also marked the high point in the religion of Yahweh is much more debatable.

As we saw in the last chapter, the settlement of the Israelite tribes in Canaan had resulted in fundamental changes to the religion acquired in the Sinai desert. This religion had been supplemented by an essentially Canaanite cult, while Canaanite beliefs about the gods El and Baal had changed how the Israelites thought about Yahweh himself. Far from being a pure, Yahwistic, monotheistic faith, their religious belief and practice was now permeated through and through with pagan ideas imported from their Canaanite neighbors. But scarcely any less of a fundamental change occurred in the tenth century BCE when the Israelites acquired a king and a royal temple. Once again, contrary to the views of the "official plot", the new ideas and practices adopted were Canaanite, not ones traceable to the revelation of Yahweh in the Sinai desert.

David and the capture of Jerusalem

Although Saul was the first Israelite king, the nation was only truly united under his successor David (about 1000 – 970 BCE). David belonged to the tribe of Judah in the south, and he succeeded in combining south and north into a united kingdom of Israel and Judah for the first time.

But David achieved something even more significant than that. Early on in his rule he captured the city of Jerusalem and made it his personal capital.[4] This event had far-reaching effects whose importance should not be underestimated. Jerusalem had previously been the independent Canaanite city state of the Jebusites, with its own well-developed religious traditions. On capturing it David essentially became its next Canaanite city king. He had a palace built by one of his city-king neighbors, Hiram of Tyre,[5] and he adopted many of the city's beliefs and practices. Far from imposing the religion of Yahweh on his new capital city, he largely slotted himself into the Canaanite religion and society that he found there. This produced a further influx of pagan ideas into Israelite faith, taking it still further away from its starting point in the desert.

Of these new ideas and practices the most important were sacral kingship, beliefs about Zion, and the Zadokite priesthood.

Sacral kingship

Although the king was never actually regarded as a god in Israel, under the influence of Jerusalemite ideas he acquired a semi-divine status. At his coronation he was adopted by Yahweh as his son, which gave him a position far transcending that of any other human being. The king was endowed with superabundant life and sat at Yahweh's right hand sharing his sovereignty. The blessings of Yahweh flowed through him to his people and the land, so that he became the main conduit between heaven and earth. And in the other direction he became the high priest of the cult, uniquely able to offer effective sacrifices to Yahweh on behalf of his people.

This relationship is colorfully displayed in the "royal psalms" of the Old Testament, some of which were used at the coronation of the king. Psalm 2, quoted at the beginning of this chapter, speaks of him ruling on Yahweh's behalf, while Psalm 110 speaks of his priesthood:

A declaration of Yahweh to my lord: "Sit at my right hand
Till I make your enemies a footstool for your feet." ...
Yahweh has sworn and will not have regrets:
"You are a priest for evermore in the succession of
Melchizedek."[6]

"Melchizedek", whom we met in Chapter 2 blessing Abraham,[7] was an earlier priest-king of Jerusalem. David adopted his role, taking on a Canaanite view of the relationship between the divine and human worlds.

Later on the earliest Christians took these psalmic references to refer to Christ, and borrowed for him the title "Son of God" originally applied to the Canaanite kings. In doing so they unwittingly incorporated a pagan element into their new religion, one completely unconnected with the original faith of Yahweh.

Zion

"The stronghold of Zion" started as the name for a fortified structure, built on Mount Zion, which was the defensive heart of Canaanite Jerusalem. It was by storming this stronghold that David captured Jerusalem to make it his capital.[8] The name was later transferred to a neighboring hill on which Solomon built his own palace and the Temple. Mount Zion was thus the symbolic center of Jerusalem, where both royal and religious power was concentrated.

At this stage in the evolution of Israelite religion Yahweh in effect migrated from Mount Sinai to take up residence on Mount Zion. No longer an idiosyncratic desert deity, he dwelt in a temple (once built) like a proper Canaanite high god, and blessed his people through his anointed king. He had joined the Israelites in their settled existence and had adapted accordingly.

As if to underline this point, from now on the Covenant that Yahweh had made with Moses in the desert was officially superseded by a new Davidic covenant. The new Yahweh, as a proper Ancient Near Eastern deity, made a covenant with the person of the king.[9] From now on it was the behavior and faithfulness of this semi-divine figure that was crucial to the nation's well-being. The whole nation was in effect mystically present in the king, rather as in the New Testament Christians were believed to be mystically present in Christ.

The priesthood

Another effect of the capture of Jerusalem was a change in the personnel of the Israelite sacrificial priesthood. This was already quite complicated, with several groups, all tracing their lineage to the time of Moses, jockeying for position.

On capturing Jerusalem David found a "Zadokite" priesthood running the royal cult of the city. (Notice the similarity of this name to Melchi-*zedek*, the priest-king already mentioned: *Zedek* was the god worshiped by the Jebusites of the city.) Rather than replacing it, David recruited this priesthood to run his own royal cult under the leadership of its priest Zadok. It later took over the running of the Temple.

The Old Testament texts allude to an ongoing power struggle between the various priesthoods. When David later lay dying, Zadok joined the movement to get his young son Solomon installed as the next king ahead of David's older and powerful son Adonijah. (Notice in passing that Adoni-*jah* is a name based on *Yah*-weh; he had been born before David captured Jerusalem. None of David's sons born in Jerusalem have Yahweh included in their name;[10] "*Solom*-on" is a name derived instead from Jeru-*salem*.) The Israelite priest Abiathar backed Adonijah,[11] but Solomon was successful, and with him the Zadokite priesthood. Zadok anointed Solomon as the next king[12] and in return Solomon appointed Zadok as high priest in place of Abiathar.[13] The Canaanite-derived priesthood was now officially confirmed as in charge, and the Israelite priesthood was displaced. Pagan priests had permanently replaced Israelite priests at the heart of the Israelite sacrificial cult. It was they who subsequently officiated at the Temple.

David and Solomon

It is interesting to compare the verdicts of the later editors of the Old Testament on Israel's two greatest kings, David and Solomon. David's actual life, as recorded in the old stories, had some pretty murky episodes. These included a lengthy civil war[14] and the cynical murder of a man whose wife he had taken in adultery.[15] However later kings are compared to David as the benchmark of wholehearted faithfulness to Yahweh,[16] and the following peon of praise is put into his mouth on his deathbed:

> Now these are the last words of David ... the declaration of the young man who was raised up on high, the anointed of the God of Jacob, the singer of Israel's psalms:
> "The spirit of Yahweh speaks by me, his word is upon my tongue ... When one rules justly over men, ruling in the fear of God, and dawns on them as the light of morning at the rising of the sun ... Just so does not my house stand with God? An everlasting covenant he has made with me, ordered in all things and secure. Will he not make to prosper my salvation and all I take pleasure in?"[17]

By contrast the editorial summing-up of Solomon is considerably less positive, despite his actual life being less questionable and his wisdom as a ruler being legendary:

> Solomon did what was evil in the eyes of Yahweh and did not wholly follow Yahweh as had David his father ... And Yahweh was angry with Solomon, because his heart had turned away from Yahweh the god of Israel ... Therefore Yahweh said to Solomon ... "I will tear the kingdom from you and give it to your servant. Nevertheless for the sake of David your father I will not do it in your day but I will tear it out of the hand of your son."[18]

The difference arises because the later editors judged the performance of a king on only one issue: whether or not he encouraged, allowed or opposed the worship of other deities alongside Yahweh. For them skill in administration, economic success and even personal morality were of secondary importance. A man was summed up exclusively on the basis of how well he kept the first Commandment: "You shall have no other gods alongside me."

The career of Solomon presented the editors with a tricky problem. Politically he was undoubtedly far-and-away the best king Israel ever had, skillfully negotiating treaties with the surrounding nations, creating a sizeable empire, and building the Temple in Jerusalem. All this implied Yahweh's blessing. However he was also clearly lax on the issue of foreign gods, which implied Yahweh's condemnation. They solved the problem by having the punishment for the latter occur after his death, with the empire fragmenting and the north splitting away to form an independent state.

Marriage, religion and politics

Once installed as king on David's death, Solomon to all intents and purposes behaved like a standard Ancient Near Eastern potentate. To secure his international position he entered into marriage alliances with the daughters of several surrounding kings, toting up (according to the editors) an impressive 700 wives to join his 300 concubines.[19] Some of these alliances were with minor adjacent countries like Moab, Ammon and Edom, which were incorporated into his empire. He also married daughters of the kings of Egypt and the Hittites, the major regional powers of the time.[20]

These marriage alliances led to a substantial influx of foreign pagan cults into Jerusalem as the wives brought their gods with them. Despite its transparent hostility, there is no reason to doubt the essential accuracy of this editorial description:

Solomon built a high place for Chemosh, the detestable thing of Moab, on the hill which faces Jerusalem; and also for Molech the detestable thing of the Ammonites. And so he did for all his foreign wives, who were burning offerings and making sacrifices to their gods.[21]

Solomon no doubt worshiped Yahweh as well, as passages like the granting to him of wisdom in a dream make clear.[22] But during his reign the capital became a place where many different deities were worshiped, and the idea of the exclusivity of Yahweh was eclipsed. In fact this seems to have been the default position of Israelite religion as a whole under the monarchy, right up to the fall of Jerusalem to the Babylonians in 587/6 BCE.

Solomon's Temple

There always were Israelite purists who rejected the whole idea of building a temple, even a temple dedicated to Yahweh. Yahweh had no temple in the desert, they reasoned, so why did he need one now? And surely the idea that he would live in a house made by human hands was impious?[23] However the overall view of the editors of the Old Testament was that the Temple was a good thing, that the loss of it to Babylonian destruction in 587/6 was a disaster, and that its rebuilding after the exile was essential to the practice of authentic Jewish religion.[24] They believed that the building of the Jerusalem Temple by Solomon was a Yahweh-sanctioned operation, one which had been denied to David only because he had been too busy fighting defensive wars.[25]

But what the editors perhaps did not appreciate was that the Temple was a thoroughly pagan construction. Comparison of it as described in the Old Testament with several contemporary temples in Syria and Palestine shows that it was indistinguishable from other sanctuaries of the same period. Like a standard Canaanite temple it had three rooms in a line. Like the temple at Hazor it had two bronze pillars at its entrance. And as the Old Testament itself says, the work was done by the craftsmen of Hiram, king of Tyre, who would have constructed it along with familiar lines.[26] In addition, the sacrificial worship going on inside was Canaanite in form, as was all Israelite worship of the time. And although as part of its dedication Solomon brought the ark into its precincts,[27] the ark itself was probably an ancient pagan cultic object. All in all it is hard to identify anything at all about the Temple with a firm connection to the Yahweh of the Sinai desert.

Scattered comments later on in the Old Testament show that the worship inside the Temple was far from directed just towards Yahweh. For example during the reforms of Josiah, some 300 years later, the following were removed from the Temple:

- vessels made for Baal, Asherah and "all the host of heaven" (that is, a variety of other heavenly beings or gods)
- an Asherah (a wooden pillar representing the Canaanite goddess Asherah)
- male cult prostitutes and their homes (which implies the practice in the Temple of a Canaanite fertility cult; possibly the female cult prostitutes were left in place?)
- women who wove hangings for Asherah
- statues of horses, plus chariots, dedicated to the sun (the sun was a common deity in the Ancient Near East)
- altars to a variety of other unnamed deities[28]

Even allowing for some development over time, it seems that the Temple was from the beginning a general sanctuary for the worship of a variety of gods, albeit with Yahweh as the chief, rather than just a home for Yahweh himself. Solomon's practice of offering sacrifice on the "high places",[29] and the presence of foreign wives in the royal palace, would make it surprising if it had been otherwise.

As was standard in Ancient Near Eastern religion, the Temple was not just a dedicated place for worship. It was intended as a "house" for Yahweh to live in, alongside the "house" or palace of the king built next door. The three-room pattern mentioned above makes this clear. The outer room was a porch, while the middle room, "the holy place", was where the sacrifices were carried out by the priests. The small inner room was a secluded space reserved as the deity's (in this case Yahweh's) private living space. In Canaanite temples this inner "holy of holies" or "most holy place" contained an image of the deity to symbolize his or her presence. In obedience to the second Commandment the Jerusalem Temple had no image of Yahweh, who thus remained unrepresented. It did, however, have a throne involving "cherubim" upon which Yahweh was thought invisibly to sit.[30]

The record in the Book of 1 Kings goes into some detail about the Temple furnishings, also provided by Hiram of Tyre's workmen. Apart from the two huge bronze pillars (with no obvious connection to Yahwistic religion at all) they included:

- decorations of pomegranates:[31] a standard fertility symbol (because of their large numbers of seeds) echoing the central Baal myth connected to the fertility of the land
- panels of bronze depicting lions, oxen and cherubim:[32] contradicting the second Commandment forbidding solid images
- a bronze sea, supported by twelve bronze oxen:[33] possibly symbolizing the mother goddess from whose body the universe was created in Ancient Near Eastern myth
- large amounts of sacrificial paraphernalia (lamps, snuffers, tongs, cups, incense dishes, fire pans and so on) for use in the cult[34]

All together, the impression gained is one of pagan (essentially Canaanite) religion. The deity of the Sinai desert by this stage seems to have been left far, far behind.[35]

Conclusion

Some of the stories preserved in the Old Testament suggest a degree of unease about the development of kingship under David and Solomon. When the people first approach the prophet Samuel to request that he appoint them a king "like all the nations", Samuel is displeased and Yahweh tells him:

It is not you they have rejected, but me they have rejected from being king over them ... Hear their voice; but you shall clearly warn them, and show them the ways of the king who will reign over them ... He will take your sons and assign them to his chariots and to be his horsemen ... and some to plow his ground and to reap his harvest ... and he will take your daughters to be perfumers and cooks and bakers ... He will take the best of your fields and vineyards and olive orchards and give them to his servants ... He will take a tenth of your flocks, and you will have to serve him. And you will cry out on that day because of your king whom you have chosen for yourselves, but Yahweh will not answer you on that day.[36]

Much of this reflects the actual experience of kingship under Solomon, when towards the end of his reign he raised forced labor and imposed crippling taxes to pay for his prestige building projects. Yet there is also here a vague unease that the whole idea of sacral kingship is not authentically Israelite, that it is an abandonment of essential features of the religion of the desert. This chapter has argued that such unease was fully justified.

6

DIVIDED KINGDOMS AND HEBREW GODDESSES

When the king heard the words of the Book of the Law he tore his clothes ... saying ... "Great is the hot anger of Yahweh that is kindled against us, because our fathers have not listened to the words of this book to do all that is required of us!" ... So (the king's servants) went to Huldah the prophetess ... And she said to them, "Thus says Yahweh the god of Israel ... 'Behold I will bring evil to this place and against its inhabitants, all the words of the book which the king of Judah has read, because they have abandoned me and burned sacrifices to other gods' ... But as to the king of Judah ... thus says Yahweh ... 'Because you bowed down and softened your heart and humbled yourself before the face of Yahweh when you heard how I spoke against this place and its inhabitants, that they should become frightful and contemptible ... you shall be gathered to your grave in peace, and your eyes shall not see all the evil which I will bring upon this place.'"[1]

The official version: Israel destroyed by unfaithfulness to Yahweh

According to the Book of 2 Kings, in about 620 BCE a momentous discovery was made in the Temple during some repair work. Hilkiah the high priest found "the Book of the Law" which had been lost and forgotten about for generations. Hilkiah gave the scroll to the royal secretary Shaphan, who read it out to King Josiah.[2] Josiah's reaction is given in the quotation above.

It becomes clear later that the Book of the Law is none other than Deuteronomy, the fifth book of the Old Testament, a book which is particularly strong in its condemnation of any worship offered to gods apart from Yahweh. According to the "official plot", the contents of this book (and doubtless of the first four books of the Old Testament as well) had been well known to David, who had taken care to follow its instructions. But over time it had been neglected and finally lost, as the worship of other gods penetrated the pure Israelite faith. Only a full-scale reformation, the rooting out of any pagan aspects of devotion, could avert the punishment which Yahweh was to inflict for the breaking of his first Commandment.

Such a reformation was indeed achieved by King Josiah, but nevertheless Yahweh had Jerusalem destroyed by the Babylonians and the people were carried off into exile. In this respect the fate of the southern kingdom of Judah echoed that of the northern kingdom of Israel which had been destroyed by the Assyrians, for the same reason, over a century earlier.

The historical reality

Most Old Testament scholars are highly skeptical of the idea that Deuteronomy was "discovered" in 620 BCE. They think this was when the book was actually written. Far from David upholding the true Yahwistic faith from which later kings gradually lapsed, they believe that the worship of the Temple had been polytheistic from the beginning, as indeed was the worship of the "high places" in the countryside. But gradually, particularly under the influence of the prophets from the ninth century BCE onwards, a stricter Yahwism gained ground. This finally achieved royal acceptance under Josiah in 620 BCE, and its manifesto, the Book of Deuteronomy, became the benchmark of true Israelite religion.

That Jerusalem fell in 587/6 BCE, shortly after Josiah's death in 609 BCE, was put down by the editors to Yahweh's judgment on the apostasy of the years between Solomon and Josiah. But in reality the kingdom of Judah paid the inevitable price of an unwise rebellion against an overwhelmingly more powerful military machine.

Israel and Judah

Following Solomon's death in about 931 BCE his empire rapidly fragmented. The usually independent kingdoms of Edom, Moab and Ammon seceded, and the greater part of the nation proper, the northern tribes, split away to form the independent state of Israel. David's successors were left ruling the tiny state of Judah, tucked away in the hill country surrounding Jerusalem.

The much larger Israel was economically stronger and geographically more exposed to influence from surrounding states. Its brief history was characterized by regular polytheistic worship, interrupted by occasional bouts of Yahweh-only extremism inspired by prophets such as Elijah. In 722/1 BCE it succumbed to the Assyrians, Samaria its capital was razed to the ground, and its ruling and educated classes were scattered throughout the Assyrian empire. All trace of them was lost permanently to view.

The much smaller and more remote Judah often escaped the attention of the great powers, and largely for that reason survived until 587/6 BCE. Once again its worship was largely polytheistic, but the Yahweh-only movement was eventually stronger there, inspired partly by the prophets Isaiah and Jeremiah. It gained the royal ear under kings Hezekiah (possibly about 715 – 687 BCE) and Josiah (about 640 – 609 BCE). Judah too eventually fell, as we have seen. The Babylonians destroyed Jerusalem and the Temple in 587/6 BCE and again carried the ruling and educated classes off into exile. But in contrast to the Assyrians, the Babylonian policy was to keep exiled groups together, so the majority of the Judeans (Jews) were taken to Babylon. Here they survived and even flourished as a distinct culture, and partly resettled their homeland some forty years later under the Persians.[3]

The prophets

The prophetic movement had enjoyed a long and complicated history in the country that was now Israel and Judah.[4] It derived apparently from two different roots:

- The "seer" (*ro'eh*), at home in the nomadic world of the desert, who proclaimed divine instructions based primarily on visions and presentiments. Seers often crafted their oracles in poetic form, which was taken as a mark of their contact with the supernatural world. They were usually solitary individuals.
- The "prophet" (*navi'*), coming from the fertility cults of the cultivated farmlands, who gave ecstatic utterance in a trance-like state. Prophets were often grouped into bands.

By the time of the divided monarchy the two forms were combined,[5] and the great prophets of the ninth century onwards showed elements of both roles.

The prophets are important to the theme of this book in two ways. Firstly, most were hostile to any worship of pagan gods alongside Yahweh. Indeed they may have started this hostility, which eventually won the day in the Judaism of the post-exilic period. With the exception of Amos, whose main theme was social justice, the consistent message of the other great prophets (such as Elijah, Hosea, Isaiah, Jeremiah and Ezekiel) was the importance of the first Commandment. Secondly, we can trace monotheism, the belief that there is only one God, directly back to the prophets. It was they who made the conceptual leap from "*Worship* no other god apart from Yahweh" to "There *is* no other god apart from Yahweh", a leap which seems so obvious to us but clearly was not at the time.

Both of these points are well illustrated in the dramatic central crisis of Elijah, the first prophetic figure about whom we have extended stories.

Elijah

El-i-jah (whose name means "Yahweh is God") was active in the northern kingdom during the reign of Ahab in the ninth century BCE. In actual fact Ahab's reign was one of considerable prosperity and stability for Israel. But the editorial summing up of his performance, as usual concentrating on only a single issue, was uncompromisingly negative:

> Ahab, the son of Omri, did evil in the eyes of Yahweh more than all that were before him ... He took as a wife Jezebel, the daughter of Ethbaal king of the Sidonians, and went and served Baal and worshiped him. He erected an altar for Baal in the house of Baal, which he built in Samaria. And Ahab made the Asherah. Ahab did more to provoke Yahweh the god of Israel to anger than all the kings of Israel who were before him.[6]

Given this we might expect the conflict between Elijah and Ahab to be told squarely from Elijah's point of view, and indeed it is. Nevertheless we can still glimpse some interesting things about religion in Israel through the account.

As the above quotation suggests, Ahab had made a skillful marriage alliance with the ruler of a powerful Canaanite state. And as with Solomon's wives, Jezebel, Ethbaal's daughter, brought her own gods with her to Ahab's new capital Samaria. She seems to have been particularly devoted to the female goddess Asherah,[7] although no doubt she honored Baal as well.

The action starts with Elijah confronting Ahab about this, saying, "As Yahweh the god of Israel lives, before whose face I stand, there shall be these years neither dew nor rain except by my word", before escaping to the desert to avoid royal retribution. There then follows a two-year drought with a correspondingly desperate famine.[8] This of course alludes to the Canaanite Baal myth. The return of Baal from the realm of Mot in the autumn was supposed to bring the rains as his gift as god of fertility. The failure of the rains on the say-so of the prophet of Yahweh was thus a direct challenge to Baal's legitimate authority: it was claiming that Yahweh, not Baal, was lord of the weather and therefore of life itself.

There then follows a dramatic showdown on the top of Mount Carmel, a holy site not far from Samaria. In the presence of King Ahab, Elijah challenges 450 prophets of Baal to a duel which will settle the matter of sovereignty. Each side is to build an altar, lay on it wood and a slaughtered bull, and then call on their god to light the fire with a bolt of lightning from the sky[9] (from a sky, note, which had been cloudless for two dry years). "The god who answers with fire, he is God,"[10] suggests Elijah. Note here the unusual choice of a bull as the sacrificial animal. Both El and Baal were regularly represented as bulls, so Elijah is deliberately giving the opposition the advantage of the use of sympathetic magic. Moreover, as the god in charge of the weather, Baal should find a lightning-strike easy to pull off.

The 450 Baal prophets fruitlessly beseech Baal to light the fire, "raving on" for the entire morning and afternoon. During this time Elijah insults their god by suggesting that he might be relieving himself in the latrine, going deaf, or having a long snooze, in other words by suggesting that he is a mere (and doddery) old man rather than a god at all.[11] Then, once they have failed, it is Elijah's turn. Deliberately making the task more difficult by drenching his bull and wood with water:

Elijah the prophet stepped up and said, "O Yahweh, god of Abraham, Isaac and Israel, this day let it be known that you are God in Israel ... Answer me, Yahweh, answer me, that this people may know that you, Yahweh, are God, and that you have turned their hearts back." Then the fire of Yahweh fell, and ate up the burnt offering and the wood and the stones and the dust, and licked up the water in the trench. And all the people saw and they fell upon their faces, and they said, "Yahweh, he is God! Yahweh, he is God!"[12]

Elijah then executes all of the Baal prophets, following which a torrential downpour breaks the two-year drought.[13] Yahweh, the true lord of the rains, shows mercy once his people turn back to him.

Stirring stuff. But what is noticeable is how little effect on the religious affairs of Israel this alleged event seemed to have. Despite having a major miracle performed before his very eyes, Ahab returned to Samaria and business continued as usual. Jezebel came after Elijah in murderous revenge, and after only a few weeks Elijah was saying, "The Israelites have forsaken your (Yahweh's) covenant, have thrown down your altars and have killed your prophets with the sword, and I, I alone, am left."[14] So in reality the described event probably represents a localized outbreak of anti-Baal sentiment, involving the murder of some Baalite prophets by Yahweh-only extremists living near Carmel. It was not, as the editors would have us believe, a turning of the whole nation and the king away from the Canaanite gods.

Notice in the story the two prophetic stresses picked out above. The implacable hostility to other gods, especially Baal, is obvious. But what readers can easily miss is the shift in religious belief implicit in the account. Up to this point there really has been no hint in the Old Testament stories that the pagan gods *do not exist*. Indeed, it is hard to see why the first Commandment should be considered so important if they do not. But here, with Elijah's insulting of Baal and the highlighting of his powerlessness in the realms in which he was allegedly supreme ruler, we find the first hint that the other gods are mere fictions. This hint was developed more and more in prophetic circles over the succeeding centuries, until it blossomed into full-blown monotheism at the time of the Babylonian exile.

Normal worship in the divided kingdoms

The editorial condemnation of Ahab, however disapprovingly expressed, probably shows us the normal situation in the state of Israel throughout much of its existence (about 931 – 722 BCE). Worship was polytheistic, both on the high places and in the royal sanctuaries, with Baal and Asherah honored alongside Yahweh. Occasionally there were short-lived and bloody outbreaks of Yahweh-only zeal, for example under Jehu.[15] But such events were localized and had little lasting effect on the religious life of the nation. Thus we repeatedly read of altars to Baal, Asherah pillars for worship of the goddess, and (polytheistic) worship on the high places, while throughout the whole period the official Yahweh shrines contained statues of bulls (see Chapter 3).

The situation in the southern kingdom of Judah was not much different, and we have already seen what was going on in the Temple. When Josiah purged the countryside, at the same time as he purged the Temple, he destroyed: a place for child sacrifice to the god Molech; high places dedicated to Anat, Chemosh god of Moab and Milcom god of Ammon; numerous Asherah poles; many idols; a number of pagan priests; and a sacred burial ground.[16]

This last item is teasingly interesting. The relevant part of the account in the Book of 2 Kings reads as follows:

Also (Josiah) demolished the altar which is at Bethel, the high place that Jeroboam ... had built ... and he broke in pieces its stones, crushing them to dust and he burned the Asherah. And Josiah turned and saw the tombs which are there on the hill. And he sent and seized the bones from the tombs and burned them upon the altar, and defiled it ... [17]

Might Josiah's hostility to these bones indicate the survival of a form of pagan worship similar to that at the British Neolithic long barrows, which contained bones from a cross section of the population for religious purposes? And might the phrase "slept with his fathers", repeatedly applied to dead kings, be more than a mere figure of speech?[18] These are intriguing possibilities, but probably unprovable.

Be that as it may, religion in both north and south during the period of the divided kingdoms was clearly polytheistic, and the editorial attempt to present this as an aberration is misleading. Yes, the seeds of monotheistic Yahwism were starting to sprout here and there, both in Israel and in Judah. But their flowers were borne only later.

Festivals and history

While evidence for the worship of the Canaanite gods is widespread in the historical books of the Old Testament, the evidence for the festivals that were held in their honor is more fragmentary and elusive. Nevertheless it seems clear that three major annual festivals were kept, all of them connected with stages of the agricultural year, and all of them Canaanite in origin:[19]

- The Feast of Unleavened Bread[20] was held in spring at the beginning of the barley harvest. It lasted seven days, during which time the first-fruits of the new crop were presented at the sanctuary. To mark a new beginning, only bread from the new grain was eaten and this was prepared without the addition of any old dough as leaven. (The old dough contained yeast that made the bread rise; the usual way of adding yeast to the new dough was by putting in some old dough containing yeast cells. "Unleavened" means "unrisen".)
- The Feast of Weeks[21] was a one-day festival at the time of the wheat harvest, some seven weeks later, when again new grain and loaves were offered at the sanctuary.

- The Feast of Ingathering was the last and greatest feast, often referred to simply as *the* feast. This is doubtless the one recorded as the annual sacrifice at Shiloh.[22] Later called the Feast of Booths,[23] it was the autumn harvest festival. At this time the whole farming community would take a week's holiday, camping out in orchards and vineyards and sleeping in huts made of branches, while the new wine flowed freely.

As one commentator notes, "in their basic form, all three of the annual festivals suggest a great deal of Canaanite fertility religion, little of worship, and nothing of Mosaic Yahwism."[24] They reflect an essentially pagan religion in tune with the cycles of nature. Yet the editors later made an attempt to remove these associations and replace them with connections to the past history of the Israelites. This was also an attempt to connect them with Yahweh rather than with the Canaanite deities. We can compare this with later attempts to "Christianize" the pagan festivals of Easter and Yule by connecting them with events in the life of Jesus.

The Feast of Unleavened Bread was connected with the Israelite feast of Passover, celebrated at about the same time in the spring. If you remember from Chapter 3, this was a pastoral feast dating from the Israelites' time as flock-herding semi-nomads before they settled in Canaan. The two were amalgamated and rooted historically in the events of the Passover night in Egypt. Thus the (apparently irrelevant) detail in the story in Exodus that the people should eat *unleavened* bread with the meat of the sacrificed lamb on that night before fleeing.[25]

The Feast of Ingathering was connected with the wilderness wanderings that followed the Exodus.[26] It was supposed to let people experience the austerity of living in temporary shelters, and thus to remember the privations of their forebears in the desert. This association was less than successful in eradicating the pagan content of the feast. As another commentator notes drily, "to judge by the torchlight dances and the water libations of the feast in New Testament times, the attempt to associate it with the Exodus failed completely."[27] Similarly one wonders how many Christians or head teachers involved in Harvest Festival celebrations at their local church or school realize that they are perpetuating a Canaanite fertility festival!

Old Testament scholars are also intrigued by a possible connection between the Feast of Ingathering and an autumn New Year festival held widely around the Ancient Near East. This was the time, they argue, when the resurrected Baal was enthroned as king after his victory over Mot in Canaan, and an Assyrian/Babylonian deity was enthroned as king for another year in the sanctuaries of Asshur and Babylon. Possibly there was also an enthronement ritual carried out at this time of year in the Jerusalem Temple? Perhaps the Davidic king played the role of Yahweh as a dying and rising god, as the Canaanite king at Ugarit might have played the role of Baal? Psalms such as 47, 93 and 96 – 99 could fit such an occasion, for example:

> God has gone up with a shout, Yahweh with the sound of a
> trumpet.
> Praise God, praise! Praise to our King, praise! ...
> God reigns over nations; God sits upon his holy throne.
>
> Sing to Yahweh a new song, for he has done extraordinary
> things!
> His right hand and his holy arm have won him victory.
> Yahweh has made known his victory,
> To the eyes of the nations he has revealed his righteousness.[28]

But it is unclear whether such an annual ritual, which would certainly provide another colorful pagan thread in the tapestry of Israelite religion, ever actually took place.

Hebrew goddesses

When Samaria fell to the Assyrians in 722/1 BCE, and Jerusalem fell to the Babylonians in 587/6 BCE, the prophets were convinced that this was Yahweh's judgment on the sin of Israel and Judah respectively. They had disobeyed him by worshiping other gods, and Yahweh had used foreign armies to exact his punishment on them.

However by no means all of the Israelites reached this conclusion. For example there was a community of Jews (that is, people from Judah) now living in Egypt. They believed that judgment had fallen upon the nation, not because it had betrayed *Yahweh*, but because it had been unfaithful to *a goddess*. A fascinating dialogue is recorded between these exiles and a prophet in the Book of Jeremiah. Jeremiah the prophet speaks first, giving the standard prophetic position, and then the people reply:

> Thus says Yahweh of hosts, the god of Israel: "You have seen all the evil that I brought upon Jerusalem and upon all the cities of Judah: behold this day they are desolated and there is no one living in them, because of the evil which they did, provoking me to anger by burning sacrifices and serving other gods which they did not know, nor you, nor your fathers. Yet I repeatedly sent to you all my servants the prophets, saying, 'Oh, do not do this abhorrent thing which I hate!' But they did not listen ... So why do you provoke me to anger with the work of your hands burning sacrifices to other gods in the land of Egypt? ... Therefore behold I will set my face against you for evil ... In the land of Egypt they shall fall, by the sword and by famine they shall be swallowed up, from the least to the greatest they shall die by the sword and by famine ..."
>
> Then they answered Jeremiah, all the men who knew their wives had burned sacrifices to other gods, and all the women who stood by, a great assembly, and all the people who lived

in the land of Egypt in Pathros: "As for the word which you have spoken to us in the name of Yahweh, we will not listen to you. But we will certainly do everything that we have vowed: burn sacrifices to the Queen of the Heavens and pour out libations to her, as we did, both we and our fathers and our kings and our princes, in the cities of Judah and in the streets of Jerusalem. For then we had plenty of food and prospered and saw no evil. But since we left off burning sacrifices to the Queen of the Heavens and pouring out libations to her, we have been in great want and have been swallowed up by the sword and by famine."[29]

The people put their misfortune down, not to a betrayal of Yahweh, but to a lack of faithfulness to the Queen of the Heavens who had withdrawn her blessings as a consequence. And they imply that the worship of this goddess had been normal throughout Judah, even being practiced by the Davidic kings themselves.

The feminine face of the divine
The Yahweh of the Old Testament was a male god. Sometimes that was denied by more philosophically inclined Old Testament writers who held that God was above earthly matters like sex and gender. But a glance at the metaphors regularly used to describe Yahweh strongly suggests that it is true: from "man of war", "lord of hosts" and "king", down to the "our father in heaven" of the New Testament. Moreover Hebrew has different male and female forms for its verbs, and the male form was always used, without exception, to describe the actions of Israel's national god.

Given this, and given the human need for a feminine aspect of the divine, it would be surprising if the Israelites had not found the need to worship goddesses as well as Yahweh. The worship of Baal and El could not satisfy that need, but the worship of Asherah and Anat could. Thus the worship of these goddesses was pervasive from the earliest times of the settlement in Canaan, despite periodic attempts by Yahweh-only extremists to stamp it out, and despite the vitriol against it found in the texts.

Asherah

The worship of Asherah by the Israelites is the better attested of the two. Pillars representing her (also called Asherim and Ashtaroth which are Hebrew plural forms) are frequently described as being present at the high places, in the capital, and even inside the Temple itself. For example:

- Gideon, a hero from before the monarchy, cut down the Asherah alongside the Baal altar of his father, and was viewed as a dangerous extremist as a result.[30]
- Samuel exhorted the people to abandon worship of Baal and Asherah, both obviously pervasive, once the ark was returned after its capture by the Philistines.[31]
- Asherah were still present in the northern capital of Samaria in the reign of Jehoahaz, despite the recent Yahweh-only purge by his father Jehu against the worship of Baal.[32]
- The people of the northern kingdom were described as having "set up for themselves pillars and Asherim on every high hill and under every green tree", contributing to the fall of Samaria to the Assyrians.[33]
- Periodic reforms involved the cutting down of the Asherah in Judah, which were presumably a normal part of worship in between.[34]
- At the time of Josiah an Asherah was present in the Temple,[35] possibly having been there from the time of Solomon's son Rehoboam.

While the occasional outbreaks of extremism had some success at rooting out Baal worship, they had much less success against devotion to Asherah.[36] Maybe the legitimate emotional and spiritual needs met by worship of the goddess simply could not be met by worship of the male Yahweh.

Apart from the biblical evidence, archaeologists have also uncovered large numbers of female figurines from the period scattered through Israelite territory. Their number suggests they were frequently present in normal households. It seems probable that these were statues of Asherah, the domestic version of the larger public pillars erected at the sanctuaries. A seventh-century BCE Hebrew text discovered in Syria beseeches the help of Asherah for a woman in delivery. So perhaps these statuettes were particularly used by the women of the family to facilitate childbirth and/or promote fertility.

At Ugarit Asherah was a motherly goddess, more approachable than her husband El. So it is quite possible that many Israelites regarded her as Yahweh's consort, and approached her to intercede for them with her fiercer partner. This would also help to explain the widespread and persistent nature of her worship. At any rate, worship of Asherah was clearly very common among the Israelites right from their settlement in Canaan down to the fall of Jerusalem some 600 years later.

Anat

As we saw in Chapter 4, Anat (also called Astarte or Ashtoreth) was a much fiercer deity than Asherah, being a goddess of war as well as of love and fertility. Although very important in the Ugarit Baal myths, her worship is less well attested in the Old Testament than the worship of Asherah. Nevertheless:

- Worship of her is cited as one reason why the kingdom fragmented after Solomon's death.[37]
- Some Israelite place names and people are named after her.[38]

- The "Queen of the Heavens", mentioned above in connection with the Jews in Egypt, was probably Anat rather than Asherah: there is evidence that Anat was given the title "Lady of Heaven" in Egypt.

If this last point is true, then the worship of Anat was widespread in Judah before the Exile.

We have further evidence of what that worship might have involved from the Book of Jeremiah:

Do you not see what they are doing in the cities of Judah and in the streets of Jerusalem? The children collect wood, the fathers kindle fire and the women knead dough to make cakes for the Queen of the Heavens.[39]

The word translated "cakes" here, *kawwanim*, is found nowhere else in the Old Testament and is probably of foreign origin. Interestingly, a Babylonian hymn to Ishtar (an equivalent goddess) mentions sacrificial cakes called *kamanu* being offered to her.

Putting both Jeremiah passages together, we can speculate that the burnt sacrifices, libations and cakes offered to Anat were believed to guarantee food and security from her in return. As a goddess of both fertility and war, she would have been well placed to provide both.[40]

7

BY THE WATERS OF BABYLON

"Comfort, comfort my people," says your God. "Speak tenderly to Jerusalem and announce to her that her forced service is completed, that her guilt is paid off, that she has received from Yahweh's hand double for all her sins" ...

Up to a high mountain, up with you, Zion, bringer of good news! ... Behold the Lord Yahweh comes with strength, and his arm rules for him.[1]

The official version: a repentant return to the true faith
According to the "official plot" of the Old Testament, Jerusalem was destroyed, and the leaders of Judah were exiled in Babylon, because of their sin. Specifically they were punished for breaking the first Commandment by worshiping other gods besides Yahweh. Over the course of the forty years spent in exile, the people repented at leisure and realized the error of their ways. They returned to their true faith, the faith revealed to Moses in the Sinai desert, and determined henceforth to worship Yahweh alone. Yahweh therefore moved the heart of Cyrus, the Persian emperor who conquered Babylon in 540 BCE, to decree that they should return home to rebuild Jerusalem and the Temple. This duly happened in 538 BCE. The prophet Isaiah celebrates this event with the words quoted above.

According to this view of history, the Exile was a time of returning to roots, not a time of creating something new. It was a return to the faith of Abraham, Moses and David, not the making of a new religion. But in reality the Exile was the most creative period of all in the formation of the Old Testament. And it was by the waters of Babylon that the great monotheistic religion of

Judaism was constructed using the building materials provided by earlier Israelite religion.

The political reality

Considered in the light of political realities, the Babylonian Exile was less a punishment for apostasy than the result of unwise political decisions on the part of the kings of Judah. Josiah's reform (see Chapter 6) had coincided with the collapse of the Assyrian empire, of which Judah had been a client state for some time. As Assyria was overwhelmed by Egyptian and Babylonian rebellions from within and invasion by Medea from without, a power vacuum allowed Josiah room for maneuver. His reform was nationalistic as well as religious: it was a bid for freedom from foreign domination. At first it was successful, but this happy state of affairs was not to last.

Following Josiah's death, Judah found itself balanced uncomfortably between the erstwhile rebels Egypt and Babylon. When the Babylonian army arrived on a campaign the Judean king of the time, Jehoiakim, unwisely joined the Egyptians in an attempt to repel them. The Babylonians won, captured Jerusalem in 597 BCE, and made Judah a vassal state under the puppet ruler Zedekiah. Zedekiah was then caught between the nationalistic prophets calling for further resistance with reliance on Yahweh's help, and the wiser counsel of the prophet Jeremiah advising submission. He plumped for the former. The expected help from Egypt failed to materialize, and the Babylonians under Nebuchadnezzar took and destroyed Jerusalem in 587/6 BCE. They deported its leaders and incorporated its territory into their empire. The Exile had begun.

The return of the exiles was also essentially a matter of politics rather than religion. In 539 BCE Cyrus the Persian entered Babylon, ending the Babylonian empire. Cyrus favored a more liberal foreign policy than his predecessors and treated the displaced peoples under his control with considerable respect.

Several exiled communities were encouraged to return home, and with them went some of the Jews, who returned to Jerusalem. The end of the Exile was thus part of a wider movement of peoples within the Persian empire, rather than a unique event organized for his people by Yahweh.

Monotheism or capitulation

The followers of Yahweh among the exiles in Babylon were faced with a clear choice: to give up or to move on. On the face of it the case for giving up was much stronger. The most obvious explanation for the fall of Jerusalem was that Yahweh had been defeated by a stronger deity, the Babylonian god Marduk. In which case Yahweh was powerless to help them. This was the explanation that most religious people at the time would have accepted, and to accept it would certainly have meant the end of Yahwism as a religion. What is the point of remaining loyal to a second-rate god if the worship of a first-rate god (Marduk) is on offer instead?

The only other possible explanation for the tragic events was that Yahweh could have helped them but had chosen not to. This in turn could only be because they had offended him in some way. The breaking of his first Commandment, "You shall have no other gods alongside me", was the obvious choice. This alternative explanation was the one accepted by the editor of the history of Israel who is usually referred to as The Deuteronomic Historian or Dtr for short. (He is given this name because his point of view is similar to that expressed in the Book of Deuteronomy.)

In the event, the viewpoint of Dtr carried the day and became Jewish orthodoxy. But it was then supplemented by another development. Picking up on the intuitions of the earlier prophets, and on the idea of El as creator derived originally from Canaanite religion, inventive thinkers started to wonder about the real status of Yahweh. Was he just a god like Marduk, or could it be that he was something even greater? Could it be that Yahweh was in fact the only true God, the Creator of the entire universe, and that all other alleged gods were merely fictions? It is hard for us to appreciate how staggeringly improbable this must have seemed to a defeated remnant exiled at the power center of the greatest world empire. But that is indeed what some of them came to believe. Their audacity is astounding.

This new monotheistic insight is contained within the writings of an unknown prophet of the time who is usually known as Deutero-Isaiah ("second Isaiah" because his writings are preserved as the second part of the composite Book of Isaiah). This chapter opens with a quotation from him, and here is another flavor of his work:

Who has measured out the waters in the palm of his hand, gauged the heavens with a span, held the dust of the earth in a measure, and weighed the mountains in a balance and the hills in scales? ... Behold, nations are like a drop from a bucket, and are reckoned as a layer of dust on scale pans ... All the nations are as nothing before him, they are reckoned by him as less than nothing and a void ... Have you not known? Have you not heard? Has it not been reported to you from the start? Have you not understood from the foundations of the earth? The one who sits above the disc of the earth, and its inhabitants are like grasshoppers, who stretches out the heavens like gauze, and spreads them like a tent to dwell in...[2]

The "nations" were primarily, of course, the mighty Babylonian empire in which the writer found himself. And the great one was Yahweh, not Marduk. This could only be believed by an act of blind faith, one which flew in the face of all the evidence. But again, remarkably, it became Jewish orthodoxy.

It was at or just after this point, once the creatorship of Yahweh had been accepted, that the creation story at the beginning of the Old Testament was written. And in it another strain of pagan influence can be detected. Up to this point the Old Testament was mainly influenced by Canaanite ideas, but now an input from the religion of Babylon becomes discernible.

The great flood

Most people are familiar with the story of Noah's ark and the animals going in two by two to escape the great flood. But few people are aware that this Old Testament story is an adaptation of an earlier Babylonian one. The Babylonian flood story is a small section of *The Epic of Gilgamesh*.[3] This is one of the earliest known works of literature in any language, and was discovered written on twelve clay tablets in the library of the Assyrian king Ashurbanipal at Nineveh. Although these date from the seventh century BCE they are based on much earlier Sumerian materials from the third millennium BCE. The similarities between the Old Testament and Babylonian versions are striking, and provide further clear evidence of the influence of pagan ideas on the Old Testament texts. This influence is most likely to have occurred during the Exile.

The Epic of Gilgamesh

The latter part of *The Epic of Gilgamesh* concerns the quest of its hero Gilgamesh for immortality following the death of his friend Enkidu. He seeks out the help of the ancient Utnapishtim, now immortal himself, who had survived a great flood in the past. Although eventually dashing Gilgamesh's hopes of immortality, Utnapishtim first tells him the story of the flood in the last tablet of the epic.

The gods had decided to send a great flood, but Utnapishtim's god Ea wanted to save him. Ea told him to build a ship, and on the ship to take the seed of all living things. Aided by the local townspeople, Utnapishtim built a huge ship with an acre of floor space and six decks. Then onto the ship he loaded his gold and silver, his family, and whatever he could find of all living things, both wild and tame. Then as the rains started to fall he boarded the ship and battened up the entrance.

A great storm arose and continued until eventually even the tops of the mountains were submerged. The townspeople were overtaken and killed, and even the gods fled back to heaven where they cowered, weeping like dogs in terror. For six days and nights the storm continued, but on the seventh it became calm. When Utnapishtim looked out of the ship all he could see was flat water. All of humankind had been killed.

Eventually the waters went down, the mountains started to emerge, and the ship came to rest on Mount Nisit. Seven days later Utnapishtim released a dove, but it returned as it could find nowhere to land. Then he set free a swallow, but it too returned. Finally he sent forth a raven, which did not return because the land had started to appear.

Utnapishtim then let all of the animals out of the ship and offered a sacrifice on the mountain. The gods smelled the pleasing odor of the sacrifice and crowded around like flies. The god Enlil, who had caused the flood, was enraged that any human being had escaped destruction. But he was placated by Ea and he touched Utnapishtim's and his wife's foreheads, making them immortal like the gods.

Noah

If you know the story of Noah and his ark from the Book of Genesis, you will have noticed an uncanny resemblance to the Babylonian story outlined above. The versions are not identical, and the reasons for the flood and the finale are different in the two cases, but the overall sequence of events and many of the details are the same.

In the Noah story, as human beings began to multiply and spread over the earth Yahweh noticed that they had become thoroughly wicked. He was sorry that he had made them at all, and resolved to wipe them out. However Noah was an exception. So Yahweh instructed Noah to build a huge ark with three decks. Onto the ship he loaded a male and female of every sort of animal (but seven pairs of "clean" animals), food, and his family. And then the flood commenced.

The rain fell for forty days and nights until all the high mountains were covered. All humankind and all of the animals were killed, except for those on the ark.

After another 150 days the water had gone down and the ark came to rest on the mountains of Ararat. Shortly afterwards the tops of the other mountains were also seen. Forty days later Noah released a raven, which went to and fro until the waters had dried up. He then set free a dove, but the dove found no place to land and returned. Later he sent forth the dove again, and this time she returned with a freshly plucked olive leaf, so that Noah knew that the waters had subsided. Finally he released the dove a third time, and she did not return.

Noah then removed the cover of the ark and saw that the ground was dry. He, his family and all the animals left the ark, and Noah sacrificed one of every clean animal on an altar. Yahweh smelled the pleasing odor of the sacrifice and resolved never again to destroy every living creature as he had just done. He put a rainbow in the sky as a sign of his agreement to this effect.[4]

Similarities and differences
The Old Testament writer or editor has clearly made use of the Babylonian story, but has changed its theological meaning. No longer is it a quest for immortality, the pursuit of which was considered impious. Instead it has become an example of the righteous judgment of Yahweh on sin. In the Babylonian version there are no convincing reasons offered as to why the gods wanted to destroy the world; it is just the sort of thing the notoriously capricious gods often did. But in the Genesis version

human beings bring the destruction upon themselves by their wickedness, just as Jerusalem had brought the destructive "flood" of the Babylonian armies upon itself by its wrongdoing. The Old Testament writer thus wants his readers to learn a moral lesson from the story, not just to be entertained.

The new writer has also tinkered with some of the details. For example you can see him deciding that a mating pair of *all* animals needs to get on board, and that Noah needs some spares for the sacrifice at the end. So extra pairs of (ritually) clean animals are taken as well. However, many common features are left the same, including these:

- the ark and the flood
- the hero's family joins him in the ark, but no one else
- the flood covers even the tops of the mountains, and all other human beings are killed
- animal life and human life are both saved on the ark, but plant life is not
- birds are released to see if the waters have receded
- a sacrifice is performed on leaving the ark
- the gods or Yahweh are pleased by the smell of the sacrifice

So one of the best-loved stories of the Old Testament has, in fact, come from a pagan source.

As to whether the original Sumerian story has any historical basis: we are dealing here with a culture living on low-lying ground between the Tigris and Euphrates rivers in the south of what is now Iraq. Flooding would have been a common occurrence, and great floods, sweeping away towns and drowning the land as far as the eye could see, must have happened on rare occasions. It would be natural for the Sumerians to assume that such a flood had engulfed the whole world; indeed it had engulfed the whole of the *known* world, which was then restricted to the flat area around the rivers.

The creation

Even more important than the flood story is the possibility of Babylonian influence on the creation stories found in the Old Testament. In actual fact there are three of these, all remarkably different:

1 The one at the beginning of the entire Old Testament at Genesis 1, involving a seven-day scheme.
2 A second one, involving Adam and Eve in the Garden of Eden, which follows immediately in Genesis 2 – 3.
3 Scattered allusions to a creative struggle with a chaos monster, found in the books of Isaiah, Psalms and Job.

The most significant Babylonian material for comparison is the creation story called *Enuma Elish*. This was also found in Ashurbanipal's seventh-century BCE library, and also has much older antecedents. The story features Marduk, the national god of Babylon, and his struggle with the personified forces of chaos in the form of the goddess Tiamat.[5]

Marduk and Tiamat

Enuma Elish tells of a battle between two groups of gods. The heroes are led by Marduk, a young god who later goes on to found Babylon. The bad gods are ranged around Tiamat, an ancient goddess personifying the raging ocean, who is wreaking havoc in the heavens.

After two older gods have failed to quell her, the young Marduk rides forth to do battle against the monstrous Tiamat. Armed with a bow and arrow, a mace and a net to ensnare her, he is filled with the power of the Lightning and is surrounded by seven winds including the Evil Wind, the Whirlwind and the Hurricane. When he catches sight of Tiamat he sends ahead the seven winds to stir up her waters into a frenzy. Then, mounted on his storm-chariot pulled by the horses Killer, Relentless, Trampler and Swift, wrapped in the armor of Terror and turbaned with a halo of Lightning, he charges towards his raging adversary.

Tiamat is stung into fury by the sight of the charging Marduk, and crying aloud utters a deadly spell to kill him. Marduk wards this off, they clash, and the god casts his net over the watery monster. The enraged Tiamat opens her great mouth to swallow him up, whereupon Marduk thrusts the Evil Wind in through her jaws and down into her belly. She swells up helplessly with the wind and Marduk releases an arrow which splits her heart. Thus is the monster slain.

To the jubilant shouts of his followers, Marduk stands upon Tiamat's carcass, crushing her skull with his mace and severing her arteries so that the watery blood rushes out. Then he splits her belly in two like a shellfish, and lifts one domed half up to form the heavens, with guards set so that its waters cannot escape to deluge the earth. From her spittle he makes the clouds, and he cuts off her head to form the great northern mountains, with the Tigris and Euphrates flowing out through her eye sockets.

To celebrate his victory he also establishes the lights in the sky. He sets up likenesses of the gods in the sky as constellations of stars, and makes the moon to keep track of the days and months by its waxing and waning.

Finally, from the rebel god Kingu, humankind is made. The other gods bind Kingu, Marduk severs his blood vessels, and humans are fashioned from his spilt blood and put to the service of the gods. Then, the work done, the victorious gods sit down to a banquet. They eat, drink and make merry.

This was an appropriate form of myth for a country like Babylon, located on the flood plain of two great rivers. Over winter the rivers flooded, submerging the fields and obliterating any traces of order. Then in spring the waters retreated, dry land emerged, and the activities of civilization could resume in a recreated cosmos. The myth personified this annual event as the primeval defeat and dividing of the chaotic waters at the beginning of the world.

The chaos monster in the Old Testament

All this sounds very different indeed from the idea of creation found in the Old Testament. But in fact there are significant parallels, at least to the third version of the creation story in Isaiah, Psalms and Job. In the Babylonian myth there is a struggle against chaos, chaos personified as a water monster. And traces of the same myth can be found in the Old Testament:

> Up! Up! Clothe yourself with strength, O arm of Yahweh!
> Arise as in ancient days, the generations of antiquity.
> Are you not he who cut Rahab in pieces, who pierced the sea
> monster?
> Are you not he who cut the sea in pieces, the waters of the
> great deep?[6]

> You divided the sea with your strength,
> You shattered the heads of the sea monsters upon the waters;
> You crushed the heads of Leviathan into pieces,
> Giving him as food to demons.
> You split open springs and brooks, you dried up ever-flowing
> streams.[7]

> With his might he stirred up the sea, with his understanding
> he beat Rahab to pieces;
> By his wind the heavens were polished, his hand pierced the
> cosmic serpent.[8]

It takes little imagination to see Rahab and Leviathan corresponding to the Babylonian Tiamat and suffering a similar fate.

Such a creation myth would not have resonated particularly with people living in a dry hill country like the Israelite territory in Canaan. In that situation it was the coming of the autumn rains to break the summer drought that was creative, not the going down of winter flood waters in spring. Such a dry setting is better captured by the Canaanite myth of Baal overcoming Mot, as we saw in Chapter 4. So it is unlikely that the Israelites adopted the third form of their creation myth before the Exile. That they adapted it from the myths of their captors in Babylon is much more likely.

Adam and Eden

The second Old Testament creation account, the one found in the second and third chapters of the Book of Genesis, is both fascinating and ancient. Here we have a creator deity who makes a model man by scrabbling in the dust and then blowing into it, who strolls in the garden in the cool of the day, whose footsteps can be heard as he walks, and from whom you can hide by getting behind a tree trunk.[9] Here too we have a Tree of Life which confers the immortality and wisdom of the gods on anyone who eats it,[10] and a mythical land of jewels "in the east": the direction of the rising sun.[11] The god in this story seems much more anthropomorphic (human-like) than the god of Sinai, and the other motifs are common enough in ancient non-Israelite mythology. So it seems likely that we are dealing here with a pagan myth, incorporated into Israelite religion before the Exile, adapted to explain why life is so hard even though it was made by a benevolent creator.[12]

There are two features of the story which suggest borrowing from Canaan rather than Babylon. Firstly the opening, which pictures a dry country where the annual rains recreate life-giving vegetation, as in the Baal-Mot myth:

On the day that divine Yahweh made earth and heavens, and all the shrubs of the field were not yet in being, and all the plants of the field were not yet sprouted, for divine Yahweh had not yet caused it to rain upon the earth ... then divine Yahweh fashioned Man of dust from the ground, breathed into his nostrils the breath of life, and Man became a living being.[13]

Secondly the paradise which Yahweh creates is a garden (the Garden of Eden) which is irrigated by four rivers.[14] This is a fitting picture of utopia in the dry Israelite hill country, but one much less so in over-watered Mesopotamia.

So, while it is likely that the Old Testament borrowed Babylonian ideas for its third creation account, it is more likely that Canaanite ideas underlie its second. Of course this still means that in both cases the Old Testament has borrowed pagan ideas (Babylonian and Canaanite respectively) to describe the creation of the world by its own god Yahweh.

The Genesis 1 creation account

But although the second and third of the creation accounts were constructed from pagan materials, surely this cannot be true of the first? Not the magisterial opening of the whole Bible, sweeping across from the "Let there be light!" to the creation of humankind and the Sabbath rest? Surely here at least we have pure Israelite inspiration and genius at work, uncontaminated by the beliefs of other religions? Or so most Christians and Jews would like to think.

But on looking at the details of this classic story, one familiar to almost all western people, it looks suspiciously as if it has drawn on the creation account in *Enuma Elisha*, on the battle between Marduk and Tiamat.[15]

Key points of the account

Genesis 1.1 – 2.4, which attributes the creation of the world to "God" (*elohim*) rather than to Yahweh as such, opens with a description of how things were before the first creative act:

> At the start of God's creating of the heavens and the earth, the earth was formless and empty, darkness was upon the face of the deep, and the spirit (or wind) of God was brooding (or blowing) over the surface of the waters.[16]

The Hebrew suggests that God finds a dark chaos and works upon it, rather than making the chaos himself in the first place. In other words, despite what many English translations imply, the idea of "creation out of nothing" is not here in the text. The second half of the extract is then ambiguous: it could be picturing either God's Spirit brooding like a mother hen over a fertile cosmic egg, or instead a violent gale whipping across the surface of a primeval ocean. Or both.

The actual creation consists in the imposing of order on this pre-existent chaos. It takes place in six steps, corresponding to the first six days of the week. In the first three steps the chaos is forced further and further back into an increasingly confined space so that a home for human flourishing can appear:

> Then God said, "Let there be light" ... And God saw that the light was good. And God separated the light from the darkness, and called the light Day and the darkness Night. Then there was twilight followed by the breaking of dawn: one day.
>
> Then God said, "Let there be a *raqia'* (a solid sheet as if of hammered metal) in the midst of the waters to separate them." So God made the *raqia'* and separated the waters underneath it from the waters above it ... And God called the *raqia'* Sky. Then there was twilight followed by the breaking

of dawn: a second day.

Then God said, "Let the waters under the sky be gathered together into one place, and let dry land appear" ... Then God said, "Let the earth sprout forth vegetation ..." and it was so ... Then there was twilight followed by the breaking of dawn: a third day.[17]

The fourth, fifth and sixth days then complete the construction of the created order, preparing the stage for the grand finale: the entry of humankind:

Then God said, "Let there be lights in the sky ... for signs and for seasons, for days and for years ... and to give light upon the earth" ... And God set them in the sky ... to rule over the day and over the night ...

Then God said, "Let the waters bring forth swarms of living creatures, and let birds fly above the earth ..."

Then God said, "Let the earth bring forth living creatures ... cattle and creeping things and beasts of the earth ..."

Then God said, "Let us make Man in our image, according to our likeness, and let them have dominion over ... all the earth" ... So God created Man in his own image ... male and female he created them. And God blessed them and said to them, "Be fruitful and multiply and fill the earth and subdue it ... And behold I have given you every plant ... for food. And to every ... (animal and bird) ... I have given every green plant for food." And it was so. And God saw everything that he had made, and behold it was very good. Then there was twilight followed by the breaking of dawn: a sixth day.[18]

The account finishes with a seventh day of rest, making the total of days up to the magical number seven which is also, of course, the number of days in the week.

Babylonian elements in the account

So that is the account as written in the Old Testament, which certainly seems very different from the battle between Marduk and Tiamat in *Enuma Elish*. But on looking closely, several parallels with the Babylonian account can be observed.

The first is the watery chaos with which the account begins. It is by forcing this chaos back, above the sky and away from the land, that space is created for humankind to flourish. But this is precisely what happens in the Marduk-Tiamat story. Marduk replaces chaos with order by "slaying the chaos monster". This is a mythological way of saying what we all know painfully from experience: that sorting a mess out and imposing order is hard work, a real "battle". The God of Genesis 1 is indeed more powerful than Marduk, and can do this simply with a word of command, but the task is the same.

Moreover the overall structure of the cosmos is identical in the two accounts. In both cases the sky is a solid barrier which is put in place to hold back a section of the primeval flood above it. It holds the waters back to stop them deluging the earth (and periodically lets a little through as rain: neither author knew about the water cycle!). The rest of the flood has been pushed back into the seas and the "waters under the earth" on which the dry land floats.

The word used to describe the primeval ocean or "deep" in Genesis 1, *tehom*, is also interesting. Many scholars have pointed out the similarity of the consonants in this word (*thm*) to those in Tiamat (*tmt*), and have wondered whether the Hebrew word is derived from the Babylonian name.

Now before carrying on, consider the likelihood of an Israelite coming up with the Genesis 1 account without suggestions from Babylonian cosmology. Remember that he comes from a milieu in which it is dry desert, not flooding water, that is hostile to human existence. Would he not be more likely to have creation associated with fertilizing rain, viewing water positively? However, if he were living on the flood plain of the Tigris and Euphrates, and was familiar with the Babylonian myths of both the flood and the creation, you could easily see him constructing a creation account along the lines of Genesis 1.

Apart from this matter of the waters, there are also a number of other points where a connection between Genesis 1 and Babylonian thought can be detected:

- The idea of the celestial bodies (sun and moon) "ruling over" day and night is Babylonian. Worship of, and interest in, the heavenly bodies was particularly advanced in Babylon. This included the use of them astrologically "for signs and for seasons", in other words for determining the auspicious times to undertake actions.
- The reasoning that neither humans nor animals would eat meat in an originally perfect paradise is unlikely to be Israelite. The rest of the Old Testament seems completely oblivious to the animal suffering caused by its sacrificial system.
- The three classes of land animal mentioned in Genesis 1 (cattle and creeping things and beasts of the earth) parallel the three types of land animal specified in the Babylonian account.
- The expression "Let *us* make humankind in *our* own image" (plural in both cases) is striking. It seems to come from an earlier form of the account where the creation was undertaken by a divine council of gods, rather than a single God as in Genesis 1.
- The term "formless and empty" in Genesis 1.2, *tohu wabohu*, is very unusual Hebrew, and looks like a trace of a pre-existing mythological story.

So, taking all this together, it seems likely that the author of Genesis 1 has heavily adapted a pre-existing Babylonian account, rather than starting from scratch with a blank sheet of papyrus. The overall theological message is certainly Israelite and monotheistic, but much of the tone coloring and detail is pagan Babylonian.

8

POLYTHEISM AND MONOTHEISM

> Perish the day in which I was born, the night which said,
> "A male child is conceived." That day, let it be darkness!
> May God not seek it from above, nor light shine upon it ...
> Why did I not come forth from the womb dead, come out
> of the belly and breathe my last? ... Why is light given to
> one in distress, and life to the bitter of soul who longs for
> death but it comes not, and digs for it more eagerly than for
> hidden treasure?[1]

It is an unwritten assumption among modern religious thinkers
that the move from polytheism to monotheism, from belief in
many gods to belief in one God, was both inevitable and was
progress. It is assumed that the world is best understood as the
mysterious work of a single creator, and that the belief in many
gods belongs to the unscientific childhood of our species.

This applies to virtually all commentators on the Old
Testament, be they conservative or be they radical, be they
Christian, Jewish or agnostic. Almost all assume, without
argument, that the polytheistic beliefs of the Canaanites,
Babylonians and Israelites were childish and misguided, and that
the monotheism of the prophets like Elijah and Isaiah was
religion coming of age. Almost all side with the editors of the Old
Testament in believing that Yahweh (however imperfectly understood) is the only true God, and that Baal and Asherah, Marduk
and Tiamat do not represent anything real or valuable.

I think they are wrong. Whatever the advantages of
monotheism, it has at least five disadvantages compared to a
more untidy polytheism. These disadvantages are: less

explanatory power, less emotional satisfaction, less grounding in nature, less encouragement for creative action and less realism about human nature. Looked at the other way around, polytheism has the five corresponding advantages.

The advantages of polytheism

Explanatory power
All monotheistic believers soon run up against "the problem of evil and suffering". This problem is one of the most profound challenges to religious belief, and goes like this:

1 God is supposed to be both all-good/loving, and all-powerful.
2 A good and loving God cannot *want* evil and suffering to exist.
3 An all-powerful God *is able to* eliminate evil and suffering.
4 But the world is full of evil and suffering.
5 Therefore an all-good/loving and all-powerful God cannot exist.

It is no use blaming evil and suffering on a Devil, because an all-powerful God could get rid of a Devil if he wanted to. Neither is it helpful to say that all suffering leads to a higher good, because a lot of it plainly does not: it is simply destructive. Nor can we say that all of suffering is an inevitable price to be paid for human free will, because this does not explain the suffering caused by natural phenomena like earthquakes and cancer. So the sincere monotheistic believer is forced back on saying that God's purposes in allowing evil and suffering are a mystery.

This is the position taken by the Book of Job in the Old Testament, written after the Exile once Jewish faith had become truly monotheistic. Job, as described in the book bearing his name, was a good man who nevertheless suffered horribly. The quotation above gives a small sample of how he felt. Because he was a good man, his suffering could not be a just punishment for sin. So why was it happening?

At the end of the book, Job asks God to justify himself, to explain why he has allowed him to suffer so much. But the only answer Job receives is this:

> Shall one who conducts a lawsuit against the Almighty correct him? ... Will you even challenge my rulings? ... Have you an arm like God's, and can you thunder with a voice like his?[2]

In other words, I am inconceivably more powerful than you, so you should not question me. To which Job, the model faithful man, responds:

> I know that you can do all things, and none of your plans are impossible for you ... I have spoken of great things which I did not understand, things too wonderful for me to know ... Therefore I withdraw and repent in dust and ashes.[3]

Job settles for regarding God's ways as a mystery beyond his comprehension, for believing that if there is an explanation for his suffering he cannot understand it. And this is precisely the position in which modern monotheistic believers find themselves when faced with their own or other people's suffering. It is a position lacking in explanatory power.

Now compare this with the perspective on evil and suffering offered by polytheism. As the gods are by no means all totally good or loving, and the good ones are not all-powerful, it comes as no surprise to the polytheist that evil and suffering exist in the world. There is no inexplicable mystery here at all. Now consider the issue backwards. If we were to start with open and inquiring minds, and looked at the world as it actually is, what sort of deity or deities would it seem to suggest? The answer is certainly not a single, wholly good and loving, all-powerful God.

Emotional satisfaction

Human beings look to their religion for ultimate fulfillment, for the satisfaction of their deepest legitimate emotional and spiritual needs. But monotheism struggles to achieve this because its God lacks the complexity of the human psyche.

This is particularly clear when it comes to the issue of gender. The western monotheisms, despite some intellectual denials to the contrary, all have an essentially male deity. So this God fails to provide the divine feminine that all human beings need on a deep psychological level. That is why the Blessed Virgin Mary provides, in effect, a female deity within Roman Catholic and Orthodox Christianity, even though her divinity is officially denied. Devotion to her is so popular because it meets a very real need.

A similar lack of the divine feminine was felt in post-exilic Judaism once Asherah and Anat had been rejected. Here it was met by the emergence of the figure of Wisdom, who became in effect a female divinity alongside Yahweh:

> Does not Wisdom call, and Insight raise her voice? On top of the heights beside the way, at the crossroads she stands; beside the gates in front of the town, at the entrance, the openings, she calls aloud: "To you, O men, I call, my call is to the sons of men ... Hear for I will speak noble things, and rightness flows from my lips ...
>
> "Yahweh created me at the beginning of his undertaking, before all else that he made long ago. From everlasting I was set up, from the start, from before the earth ... When he established the heavens I was there, when he drew a circle on the face of the deep ... I was beside him as a craftsman, I was his delight day by day, rejoicing before his face always."[4]

This figure of Wisdom, *hokma* in Hebrew, is feminine. In the above passage she comes close to being presented as Yahweh's female consort, just as Asherah had been the consort of El in Canaanite religion.

But while in monotheism the divine feminine has to be smuggled in through the back door, in polytheism she can enter through the front door on an equal footing to the masculine. Moreover polytheism can accommodate the various complex aspects of the human unconscious which Jung identified as Archetypes. Each of these can be personified in the form of a different deity, including the less savory ones. This approach makes it straightforward to use polytheistic religion for psychological development.[5] But monotheism denies legitimacy to many aspects of the psyche that need to be expressed, honored and integrated, regarding them as merely sinful.

Grounding in nature
Monotheism, at least as it has developed in the west, draws a sharp distinction between God on the one hand and the universe he has created on the other. There is no question of identifying God with nature as occurs in pantheism. God is transcendent and detached from his creation, not immanent in it.

This lack of the divine in nature has two unfortunate consequences. The first is that we see the "real" world as the one which is attained in heaven after death, while the present world is devalued. It becomes a mere ante-room, a "vale of soul-making", where the soul suffers awhile before entry into the consummation of the future. The second consequence is that we see the physical world as lacking in ultimate value, as something which it is acceptable merely to exploit for our own ends.

There is currently a considerable effort by Christian thinkers to deny this and to see our appropriate relationship to the natural world as one of "stewardship". We were given the created order to "look after", so the argument goes, not to trash. Like a gift from a favorite aunt, the world is precious because of its giver; it would be disrespectful of us to ruin it. Christians should therefore support environmental projects, should be "green", because of their faith.

Such an argument is implicitly, and sometimes explicitly, based on the creation story in Genesis 1. But it has to be said that that story offers little support for such a position. The words used for having "dominion" over the animals and "subduing" the creation in Genesis 1.28, *rathah* and *kavash*, are regularly used elsewhere in the Old Testament for enslaving people, raping women and treading down enemies in battle. They are not the gentle "caring for" words which Christian thinkers would like to find there. Moreover, at best "stewardship" encourages a paternalistic care for something to which we feel superior, rather than a recognition that we are just one part in something greater than ourselves. At least one influential writer has therefore traced our western ecological crisis to the sentiments contained in this passage.[6]

The approach of pagan polytheism is in stark contrast at this point. Frequently seeing the deities as personifications of the forces of nature, it encourages an attitude of reverence and respect for the natural world as an integral part of faith, not as a bolt-on extra. From the ancient Israelite celebrating the agricultural festivals and joining in re-enactments of the Baal-Mot myth, to the modern pagan attuning to the elements and the cycle of the seasons, pagan polytheism encourages the feeling that we are part of a divine nature, not a divorced overlord of a mere mechanical machine.

Scope for creative action

Now of course it is true that Judaism, Christianity and Islam all strongly encourage action. All maintain that behavior towards one's neighbor is at least as important as religious belief, if not more so. Christian saints such as Mother Teresa and Martin

Luther King, to look no further, make this abundantly clear and were truly inspirational in how they lived their lives.

However, this action is on the social level, concerning how we treat other people, not "religious" action as such. It is in tune with the spirit of the prophet Amos of the eighth century BCE:

> I hate, I reject your pilgrim-festivals, and I will not suffer the smell of your sacred ceremonies. Even though you offer me your burnt offerings and cereal offerings I will not accept them ... Take away from me the noise of your songs; to the music of your stringed instruments I will not listen. But let justice flow down like waters and righteousness like an ever-flowing stream.[7]

For the monotheist, the correct approach in the religious realm is one of quiescence and acceptance, of waiting for God to move and not twisting his arm, of accepting whatever happens as God-given. "Yet not what I will, but what you will", as Jesus classically said in the Garden of Gethsemane on the night before the Crucifixion.[8]

Pagan polytheism, by contrast, gives a much more positive reception to magic: religious actions designed to change the world (including the practitioners' mental and emotional states) in accordance with their will. Such practices are at best grudgingly given house room as "folk religion" by Christianity, but they are welcomed and integrated fully into polytheistic paganism. This enables the polytheistic believer to work towards changing themselves and their world using a gamut of creative spiritual techniques denied to the consistent monotheist.

Realism about humanity
Finally, it is clearly the case that the gap between human ideal and human actuality is almost unbridgeable in the monotheistic religions. To take Christianity as the most extreme example: the

ideal is to love your enemies as well as your friends.[9] However the actual history of the faith shows remarkably few Christians living this out in practice. The result can be a nagging sense of failure and guilt, a preoccupation with sin, and a disincentive to wholeheartedly joyful living.

Pagan polytheism by contrast does not set out with such impossibly high ideals. Human beings as they are is the starting point, not human beings as ideally they should be. The huge gap between the perfectly righteous and disappointed God and the miserably sinful and guilt-ridden human being is not present. The ethical ideal is generally a version of the golden rule: to treat others as you would wish to be treated yourself.[10] And while this is certainly difficult to achieve in practice, it is not impossible. We do, after all, teach it to our children and expect them to adopt it in their relationships with siblings and classmates. As a result, religious life within polytheistic paganism can be one of joyful discovery, rather than one of continual and demoralizing failure. And the focus can shift from an undue emphasis on sin and forgiveness to stress a more creative growth and discovery.

Re-evaluating the pagan roots

In this book I have argued that much of the religion of the Old Testament is a polytheistic paganism rather than a strict ethical monotheism. I have also suggested that quite a lot of the content of the monotheistic God that emerges within it has been derived from pagan sources.

Although this will probably come as a surprise to most of my readers, it is a reading of the Old Testament which is widely accepted among leading scholars in European and North American universities. In that sense this book contains nothing new. What is new is my appeal for a re-evaluation of this situation. Rather than regarding the infiltration of pagan ideas as an unfortunate contamination of the true faith, I see it as positive. Rather than siding with the very vocal prophets, I am siding with the "silent majority", represented perhaps by the Jewish men and their wives who confronted Jeremiah in Egypt.

The Old Testament can be, and has been, read in many different ways by many different people over the centuries. I am suggesting it can be read for insight into the pagan roots of the modern monotheistic religions, roots which are strong, nourishing, far-reaching and full of potential in their own right.

NOTES

The Old Testament quotations in this book are the author's own translations from the original Hebrew.

1. Introduction

1. Genesis 15.1-17. The Old Testament is divided into 39 "books", of which Genesis is the first. Each book is divided into "chapters" and each chapter into "verses" to aid navigation by the reader. So "Genesis 15.1-17" means "the Book of Genesis, chapter 15, verses 1 to 17". These numbers were not in the original texts and have been added later. The Tanakh reckons the same material to be divided into 24 books because, for example, the twelve shorter prophetic writings are combined into a single book. The Christian names for the books have been used where these differ from the names traditionally used in Judaism.

2. Roman Catholic, Greek and Slavonic Bibles include some extra books that are omitted from the Tanakh and Protestant Bibles. These are usually called the Deuterocanonical Books or the Apocrypha.

3. In the Hebrew of the Old Testament the name of Israel's God is spelled *YHWH* or *yhwh* without any vowels (ancient written Hebrew had no separate capital letters, and originally had no vowels either). Later Jews regarded this name as too sacred to pronounce, so when reading the scriptures out loud they substituted the title "Adonai" (Lord) and said that instead. Many English translations of the Bible follow this convention by translating *yhwh* as "lord", but they signal that the Hebrew text has *yhwh* by rendering it "LORD" with all capital letters. We are not sure how *yhwh* was originally pronounced. In previous centuries it was thought to be pronounced "Jehovah", hence that antiquated

name for the Old Testament god. Most modern scholars (on the basis of evidence from Greek and Samaritan sources) think the pronunciation was closer to "Yahweh". This is the translation used in the Jerusalem Bible of 1966, and I have followed that convention in this book.

4. According to the texts, Abram was renamed Abraham when he was adopted by Yahweh as his worshiper.

5. See The Pagan Federation (2011) Introduction to Paganism, available from: http://www.paganfed.org/paganism.shtml (accessed 3 October 2011).

2. The Religion of the Patriarchs

1. Genesis 14.17-20.

2. "Patriarchal" can also mean "male-dominated". The term is not used in that sense here, but it is true that Abraham, Isaac and Jacob/Israel were very much in charge, with their wives having subordinate roles. This was usual in the whole of the Ancient Near East at the time.

3. Jacob has his spiritual experiences in the center of the country at the major shrines of Shechem, Bethel and Penuel. Abraham, although passing through Shechem and Bethel, is settled in the south of the country. He has his experiences at the shrine of Mamre near Hebron. Isaac operates even further south at the major pilgrimage shrine of Beer-sheba on the border of the desert.

4. *'ab 'adam* ("father of men") is identical in the Canaanite of the Ugarit texts and the Hebrew of the Old Testament. The two languages are in fact very similar, and Hebrew can be viewed as a dialect of Canaanite. Note the word *'adam* meaning "man" or "men": the "Adam" of the Old Testament Garden of Eden myth is a personification of the general idea of "mankind".

5. Genesis 31.42. *elohe* is the Hebrew "construct form" of the noun *el*, which corresponds to the genitive case in other

languages. It means "god of ...".

6. Genesis 31.42.
7. Genesis 49.24.
8. Genesis 49.24.
9. Genesis 14.18.
10. Genesis 16.13.
11. Genesis 17.1.
12. Genesis 21.33.
13. Genesis 31.13. *beth-el* means "house of God/El", the name of an important shrine in the center of the country.
14. Genesis 18.
15. Genesis 28.10-19.
16. Genesis 32.22-32.

3. Yahweh, Mount Sinai and Moses

1. Exodus 19.1-19.
2. The first five books of the Old Testament are Genesis, Exodus, Leviticus, Numbers and Deuteronomy. Judaism calls these books collectively the Torah (Law), while Old Testament scholars often refer to them as the Pentateuch.
3. In Egyptian names "ms" stands for "son of" a deity. Compare "Ra-mses", son of the god Ra; "Thut-mose", son of the god Thut/Thoth.
4. For example in Judges 6 – 7 where the Midianites defeat them in battle.
5. Exodus 3.1-14. The last paragraph is obscure and may be a play on words. *hyh* is the Hebrew verb "to be", which is close to the Hebrew for Yahweh, *yhwh*. So Yahweh's name is possibly being suggested to mean "the being one". The name is also variously interpreted as meaning "the falling one" (the god of lightning), "he who creates", "preserver", "I will passionately love whom I will love", "O He!" (as a cultic shout) and many other things. It is probably best just to regard it as the proper name of the Israelite national god.

See Fohrer, Georg, *History of Israelite Religion* (London: SPCK, 1973) pages 75 – 77. On the original pronunciation of *yhwh*, see Chapter 1 note 3.

6. The different editors prefer different names for this place. J prefers the name Sinai, while D favors Horeb.

7. In Judges 1.16 Jethro, Moses' father-in-law, is said to be a Kenite rather than a Midianite. Descriptions of the tribal groupings of the area are variable in the Old Testament, so the two groups may be partially or wholly equivalent.

8. There is considerable doubt about exactly where this holy mountain (Sinai/Horeb/the mountain of God) might be. Christian tradition locates it right at the south of the Sinai Peninsula where the Monastery of St Catherine has been built at its foot. But the tradition locating it here dates from only the fourth century CE, and most scholars favor a more northerly location, not far south of Canaan. This is a more likely location for the holy shrine of the pastoral Midianites.

9. Exodus 18.7-12.

10. Judges 5.2-31.

11. 1 Kings 19.2-15.

12. Genesis 1.27.

13. Exodus 3 – 4.

14. Exodus 5 – 15.

15. Exodus 16 – 18.

16. Exodus 19 – 40, Leviticus, and Numbers 1 – 9.

17. Numbers 9 – 36.

18. See Hutton, Ronald, "The New Old Paganism" in *Witches, Druids and King Arthur* (London: Hambledon Continuum, 2003) pages 98 – 106 for a useful summary of the arguments.

19. See Hutton (as above) pages 110 – 112, for a useful summary of the distinctive nature of Egyptian magic.

20. Exodus 4.2-4 and 4.20.

21. Exodus 7.10-12. A different Hebrew word is used here for "serpent" than was used for "snake" in Exodus 4.

22. Exodus 7.19-21.
23. Exodus 14.16.
24. Numbers 20.2-11.
25. Exodus 17.9-13.
26. Noth, Martin, *Exodus: A Commentary* (London: SCM, 1962) page 142.
27. Numbers 21.6-9.
28. Compare here a later story, in 1 Samuel 6, where a Philistine city is afflicted with tumors. It is relieved when its citizens make golden models of the tumors to turn away the power causing them.
29. 2 Kings 18.1-4.
30. John 3.14-15.
31. Exodus 4.24-26.
32. So Noth (as above) pages 49 – 50.
33. Exodus 12.21-32. The "hyssop" in the passage is not the familiar medicinal herb, but *Origanum mani* which grows on walls and was used as a sprinkling brush.
34. So Noth (as above) pages 88 – 91. This suggestion is strengthened by interpolation of instructions for an annual festival at Exodus 12.1-28 and 12.43-51 which breaks up the narrative action.
35. The Septuagint (LXX) is a translation of the Hebrew Old Testament into Greek made in Alexandria between about the third century BCE and the first century CE. It is so called because of the tradition that seventy scholars were involved in the work.
36. Exodus 14.5-31.
37. Exodus 19.20-21 and 20.18-19.
38. Exodus 20.3-17.
39. For these interpretations of the second and third Commandments see Noth (as above) pages 162 – 163.
40. Exodus 32.1-5.
41. 1 Kings 12.26-29.

4. Religion in Canaan before King David

1. 2 Samuel 6.3-7. Someone's "nose glowing hot" is standard Hebrew idiom for them getting angry. Hebrew is a concrete language which usually describes what you can actually see.

2. For detailed laws see especially Exodus 21 – 23, Leviticus 17 – 27, and Deuteronomy 5 and 17 – 25. For details about religious observance see especially Exodus 25 – 30 and 35 – 40, Leviticus 1 – 16, Numbers 6 – 8, and Deuteronomy 12 – 16.

3. Joshua 10.40 and chapters 13 – 21.

4. Judges 1.

5. The battles and other events concerning Joshua all take place in a small part of the central belt near Jericho.

6. Some other scholars favor a "peasants' revolt" model, suggesting that the Israelites were dispossessed elements displaced from the Canaanite towns who recruited the disadvantaged peoples of the countryside. See Gottwald, Norman K, *The Tribes of Yahweh: A Sociology of the Religion of Liberated Israel 1250 – 1050 BCE* (Grand Rapids: Eerdmans, 1965).

7. For an account of the site, and a translation of many of the epic texts, see Gibson, J C L, *Canaanite Myths and Legends* (London: T & T Clark, 2004). For an overview of Canaanite society and religion, see Gray, John, *The Canaanites* (London: Thames & Hudson, 1964).

8. See Gibson (as above) pages 14 – 17.

9. For an account of Canaanite religion see Gray (as above) pages 119 – 138, and Heaton, E W, *The Hebrew Kingdoms* (London: Oxford University Press, 1968) pages 44 – 48.

10. Psalm 19.1-6 and Psalm 68.5-6. The word for God in the first line of the first quotation is *el*, rather than the usual *elohim*.

11. Psalm 68.4.

12. Psalm 29.

13. 1 Samuel 1.21.

14. 1 Samuel 1.3, 1.11 and 1.24.

15. 1 Samuel 2.13-16.
16. 1 Samuel 2.18.
17. 1 Samuel 9.6-9.
18. 1 Samuel 9.13 and 9.24-25.
19. Judges 21.19-21.
20. 1 Samuel 14.40-44. Several lines are missing from the Hebrew text here, and have been restored from the Greek of the Septuagint.
21. For example 1 Samuel 2.18.
22. 1 Samuel 28.3-20.
23. Judges 11.30-39.
24. Genesis 22.1-19
25. See for example 2 Kings 3.26-27 where the king of Moab sacrifices his son in desperation when attacked by Edom. This is very similar to events at Carthage, where the desperate population sacrificed their children as a last-ditch attempt to avoid annihilation by the besieging Roman armies. The atmospheric place where this happened can still be visited in modern Tunis.
26. Joshua 3.3-17.
27. 1 Samuel 5.1-5.
28. 1 Samuel 5.6-7.
29. 1 Samuel 6.13-16 and 6.19.
30. 2 Samuel 6.6-7.
31. 1 Samuel 4.5-8.
32. 1 Samuel 4.12-22.
33. 2 Samuel 6.12-15.
34. See Exodus 25.10-22 and Deuteronomy 10.1-5 among several other passages.
35. For a good survey of the problem of the ark, see Fohrer, Georg, *History of Israelite Religion* (London: SPCK, 1973) pages 108 – 110.

5. Jerusalem, King and Temple

1. Psalm 2.4-8.
2. See for example Luke 1.31-33.
3. The reigns of David and Solomon coincided with a low point in the fortunes of the great world powers of the region which allowed space to establish an independent nation. Subsequently the Israelites were almost always in some form of politically subservient role to the empires of Egypt, Assyria, Babylon, Persia, Greece or Rome.
4. 2 Samuel 5.1-10.
5. 2 Samuel 5.11.
6. Psalm 110.1 and 110.4.
7. Genesis 14.17-20.
8. 2 Samuel 5.7.
9. For example 2 Samuel 23.5.
10. For David's sons see 2 Samuel 3.2-5 and 5.13-16.
11. 1 Kings 1.5-8.
12. 1 Kings 1.32-40.
13. 1 Kings 2.35.
14. 2 Samuel 13 – 18.
15. 2 Samuel 11 – 12.
16. For example 1 Kings 15.3.
17. 2 Samuel 23.1-5.
18. 1 Kings 11.6-12. On Solomon's wisdom see 1 Kings 3.3-28 and 10.1-10.
19. 1 Kings 11.3.
20. 1 Kings 3.1 and 11.1.
21. 1 Kings 11.7-8.
22. 1 Kings 3.5-14.
23. For example 2 Samuel 7.1-7.
24. For example Ezra 3.
25. 1 Kings 5.1-7.
26. 1 Kings 5 – 7.
27. 1 Kings 8.6-7.

28. 2 Kings 23.4-12.
29. 1 Kings 3.3-4.
30. 1 Kings 8.6-7.
31. 1 Kings 7.42.
32. 1 Kings 7.27-30.
33. 1 Kings 7.23-26.
34. 1 Kings 7.38-50.
35. Interestingly, we have evidence of at least three other temples built by the Israelites from the sixth century BCE onwards, despite the official position that Yahweh had chosen (only) Jerusalem as the place for his name to dwell. Two were built by groups of Israelites in Egypt: one at Elephantine and one at Leontopolis. The other was built by the Samaritans (the successors of the inhabitants of the northern kingdom) at Garizim. They claimed that Garizim, not Jerusalem, was the site chosen by Yahweh for his dwelling. It was destroyed in 129 BCE. For details on these temples see Vaux, Roland de, *Ancient Israel: Its Life and Institutions* (London: Darton, Longman & Todd, 1965[2]) pages 339 – 343.
36. 1 Samuel 8.4-18.

6. Divided Kingdoms and Hebrew Goddesses

1. 2 Kings 22.11-20.
2. 2 Kings 22.3-10.
3. For the history of this period see Soggin, J Alberto, *A History of Israel: From the Beginnings to the Bar Kochba Revolt, AD 135* (London: SCM, 1984) pages 189 – 257.
4. For an account of the history and nature of prophecy, see Fohrer, Georg, *History of Israelite Religion* (London: SPCK, 1973) pages 223 – 291.
5. 1 Samuel 9.9.
6. 1 Kings 16.30-33.
7. 1 Kings 18.19.

8.   1 Kings 17.1-3 and 18.1. "In the third year" means after two years, because the Israelites started counting from one, not zero.

9.   1 Kings 18.17-24.

10.   1 Kings 18.24.

11.   1 Kings 18.25-29.

12.   1 Kings 18.36-39.

13.   1 Kings 18.40-46.

14.   1 Kings 19.10.

15.   2 Kings 9.14 – 10.28.

16.   2 Kings 23.10-24.

17.   2 Kings 23.15-16.

18.   See for example 1 Kings 11.43. On the British Neolithic long barrows see Hutton, Ronald, *The Pagan Religions of the Ancient British Isles: Their Nature and Legacy* (Oxford: Blackwell, 1991) pages 19 – 44.

19.   On Israelite festivals see de Vaux (as above) pages 484 – 517.

20.   For example Exodus 23.14-15 and Leviticus 23.9-14.

21.   Exodus 34.22 and Leviticus 23.15-21.

22.   1 Samuel 1.3.

23.   Deuteronomy 16.13.

24.   Heaton, E W, *The Hebrew Kingdoms* (London: Oxford University Press, 1968) pages 137 – 138.

25.   Exodus 12.8.

26.   Leviticus 23.39-43, compare Nehemiah 8.13-18.

27.   Heaton (as above) page 139.

28.   Psalm 47.5-8 and 98.1-2.

29.   Jeremiah 44.1-18.

30.   Judges 6.25-32.

31.   1 Samuel 7.3-4.

32.   2 Kings 13.6.

33.   2 Kings 17.10.

34.   For example 1 Kings 15.13 (Asa) and 2 Kings 18.4 (Hezekiah).

35.   2 Kings 23.6.

36. For example, Jehu's reform in the north attacked the Baal altars, but there is no mention of removal of the Asherah. On Mount Carmel Elijah kills the prophets of Baal, but not the prophets of Asherah who were also supposed to be there.

37. 1 Kings 11.26-33.

38. For example the town Anathoth near Jerusalem (1 Kings 2.26) and the man Anathoth from after the Exile (Nehemiah 10.19).

39. Jeremiah 7.17-18.

40. For an extended account of goddesses in the Old Testament period see Patai, Raphael, *The Hebrew Goddess* (Detroit: Wayne State University Press, 1990[3]) pages 25 – 95.

7. By the Waters of Babylon

1. Isaiah 40.1 and 40.9-10.

2. Isaiah 40.12-22.

3. See Dalley, Stephanie (trans.), *Myths from Mesopotamia: Creation, The Flood, Gilgamesh, and Others* (Oxford: Oxford University Press, 2000[2]) pages 39 – 135.

4. Genesis 6 – 9. Inconsistencies in the text suggest that the Genesis account contains two or more versions of the story which have been combined together.

5. See Dalley (as above) pages 228 – 277.

6. Isaiah 51.9-10.

7. Psalm 74.13-15.

8. Job 26.12-13. See also Psalm 89.9-10 and Isaiah 27.1.

9. Genesis 2.7 and 3.8-9. Genesis 2.4b-25 (the creation) and Genesis 3 (the fall) are two parts of a single story written by the same author.

10. Genesis 2.9 and 3.22.

11. Genesis 2.8 and 2.11-12.

12. Hence the curses on the man, the woman and the serpent for having disobeyed Yahweh: Genesis 3.14-19.

13. Genesis 2.4-7. The Hebrew word translated "Man" here is

'adam. Hence the idea that the man in the Garden of Eden was called Adam.

14. Genesis 2.8-15. The rivers include the Tigris and Euphrates. From a Canaanite perspective these are to the east and part of a well-watered, semi-legendary paradise.

15. The work which first suggested this at length is Gunkel, Hermann, *Creation and Chaos in the Primeval Era and the Eschaton: A Religio-Historical Study of Genesis 1 and Revelation 12* (Grand Rapids: Eerdmans, 2006; first German edition 1895). It remains a classic and is still in print in paperback form. For a modern interpretation along similar lines see Armstrong, Karen, *In the Beginning: A New Interpretation of Genesis* (London: Vintage Books, 2011) pages 9 – 12. The rest of this book also gives some very thought-provoking interpretations of the other Genesis stories.

16. Genesis 1.1-2. The New Revised Standard Version (NRSV) has "In the beginning when God created the heavens and the earth ..." which suggests creation out of nothing. However it gives the alternative reading as a footnote. The first word in the Hebrew, *bereshith,* is a "construct form" which means "In the beginning of ..." This is closer to the translation I suggest in the text.

17. Genesis 1.3-13.

18. Genesis 1.14-31. The Hebrew word translated "Man" here is *'adam,* as in Genesis 2.

8. Polytheism and Monotheism

1. Job 3.3-21.

2. Job 40.2 and 40.8-9.

3. Job 42.2-6.

4. Proverbs 8.1-6 and 8.22-30.

5. See for example Williams, Jean M and Cox, Zachary, *The Gods Within: The Pagan Pathfinders Book of God and Goddess Evocations* (London: Moondust Books, 2008).

6. See White, Lynn T, "The Historical Roots of our Ecologic Crisis" in *Machina ex Deo: Essays in the Dynamism of Western Culture* (Cambridge MA: MIT, 1968) pages 75 – 94.

7. Amos 5.21-24.

8. Mark 14.36.

9. Matthew 5.43-48 and Luke 6.27-31.

10. The Wiccan Rede, "An it harm none, do what ye will" is consistent with the golden rule. We do not want to be harmed by others, so we should not harm them.

FURTHER READING

For an introduction to the Old Testament as studied at university level, see Richard Coggins, *Introducing the Old Testament* (Oxford: Oxford University Press, 2001²).

On the history of the Israelites and Jews, from the beginning right through to after New Testament times, see Alberto Soggin, *A History of Israel: From the Beginnings to the Bar Kochba Revolt, AD 135* (London: SCM, 1984). Bernard Anderson's *The Living World of the Old Testament* (Harlow: Longman, 1988⁴) provides an alternative account that is more inclined to believe the version presented by the Old Testament editors themselves.

Susan Niditch, *Ancient Israelite Religion* (New York: Oxford University Press, 1997) is a modern attempt to reconstruct what Israelite religion was like before the Exile. It is inclined to look for the similarities between this and later Judaism, whereas I have stressed the differences. An older but excellent account of the same ground is Georg Fohrer's *History of Israelite Religion* (London: SPCK, 1973). Virtually any topic connected with Israelite religion can be looked up in Roland de Vaux's *Ancient Israel: Its Life and Institutions* (London: Darton, Longman & Todd, 1965²). It is a brilliantly succinct summary of a vast amount of material, but I would not recommend trying to read it from cover to cover.

The Canaanite myths from Ugarit can be found in translation in J C L Gibson, *Canaanite Myths and Legends* (London: T & T Clark, 2004). Raphael Patai, *The Hebrew Goddess* (Detroit: Wayne State University Press, 1990³) is a wide-ranging study of feminine aspects of deity in the Old Testament and later Judaism. The classic account of Babylonian influences on the Old Testament is

Hermann Gunkel's *Creation and Chaos in the Primeval Era and the Eschaton: A Religio-Historical Study of Genesis 1 and Revelation 12* (Grand Rapids: Eerdmans, 2006; first German edition 1895), while the Babylonian myths themselves can be found in translation in Stepanie Dalley (trans.), *Myths from Mesopotamia: Creation, The Flood, Gilgamesh, and Others* (Oxford: Oxford University Press, 2000^2).

For detailed historical maps, and much other fascinating and useful information besides, see Adrian Curtis (ed.), *Oxford Bible Atlas* (Oxford: Oxford University Press, 2007^4).

For a masterly broad-brush look at the evolution of the idea of "God" over the millennia, see Karen Armstrong's *A History of God from Abraham to the Present: The 4000-year Quest for God* (London: Vintage, 1999).

E W Heaton, *The Hebrew Kingdoms* (London: Oxford University Press, 1968) is an excellent read and also offers brief commentaries on several of the key biblical texts. Raymond Brown and others (eds), *The New Jerome Biblical Commentary* (London: Geoffrey Chapman, 1989) is an extraordinarily good one-volume commentary on all of the Bible books, edited by Roman Catholic scholars.

Finally, almost anything you come across written by the great (German) masters of the early flowering of Old Testament studies will be both exciting and thought-provoking, if a little difficult to penetrate at times. This includes works by von Rad, Noth and Alt.

BIBLIOGRAPHY

Ackroyd, Peter R, *Exile and Restoration: A Study of Hebrew Thought of the Sixth Century BC* (London: SCM, 1968).

Alt, Albrecht, *Essays on Old Testament History and Religion* (Oxford: Basil Blackwell, 1966).

Anderson, Bernard W, *The Living World of the Old Testament* (Harlow: Longman, 1988[4]).

Armstrong, Karen, *A History of God from Abraham to the Present: The 4000-year Quest for God* (London: Vintage, 1999).

Armstrong, Karen, *In the Beginning: A New Interpretation of Genesis* (London: Vintage Books, 2011).

Brown, Raymond E, Fitzmyer, Joseph A and Murphy, Roland E, *The New Jerome Biblical Commentary* (London: Geoffrey Chapman, 1989).

Coggins, Richard, *Introducing the Old Testament* (Oxford: Oxford University Press, 2001[2]).

Curtis, Adrian (ed.), *Oxford Bible Atlas* (Oxford: Oxford University Press, 2007[4]).

Dalley, Stephanie (trans.), *Myths from Mesopotamia: Creation, The Flood, Gilgamesh, and Others* (Oxford: Oxford University Press, 2000[2]).

Driver, Samuel Rolles, *Notes on the Hebrew Text of the Books of Samuel* (Oxford: Clarendon Press, 1890).

Elliger, K and Rudolph, W, *Biblia Hebraica Stuttgartensia* (Stuttgart: Deutsche Bibelstiftung, 1967/77).

Fohrer, Georg, *History of Israelite Religion* (London: SPCK, 1973).

Gibson, J C L, *Canaanite Myths and Legends* (London: T & T Clark, 2004).

Gottwald, Norman K, *The Hebrew Bible: A Socio-Literary Introduction* (Philadelphia: Fortress Press, 1985).

Gottwald, Norman K, *The Tribes of Yahweh: A Sociology of the Religion of Liberated Israel 1250 – 1050 BCE* (Grand Rapids:

Eerdmans, 1965).

Gray, John, *The Canaanites* (London: Thames & Hudson, 1964).

Gunkel, Hermann, *Creation and Chaos in the Primeval Era and the Eschaton: A Religio-Historical Study of Genesis 1 and Revelation 12* (Grand Rapids: Eerdmans, 2006). First German edition 1895.

Gunkel, Hermann, *Israel and Babylon: The Babylonian Influence on Israelite Religion* (Eugene OR: Wipf and Stock, 2009). Original German edition 1903.

Hayes, John H, and Miller, J Maxwell (eds), *Israelite and Judaean History* (London: SCM, 1977).

Heaton, E W, *The Hebrew Kingdoms* (London: Oxford University Press, 1968).

Holladay, William L, *A Concise Hebrew and Aramaic Lexicon of the Old Testament* (Leiden: E J Brill, 1971).

Hutton, Ronald, *The Pagan Religions of the Ancient British Isles: Their Nature and Legacy* (Oxford: Blackwell, 1991).

Hutton, Ronald, "The New Old Paganism" in *Witches, Druids and King Arthur* (London: Hambledon Continuum, 2003) pages 87 – 135.

Lang, Bernard, *The Hebrew God: Portrait of an Ancient Deity* (New Haven: Yale University Press, 2002).

Niditch, Susan, *Ancient Israelite Religion* (New York: Oxford University Press, 1997).

Noth, Martin, *Exodus: A Commentary* (London: SCM, 1962).

Noth, Martin, *Numbers: A Commentary* (London: SCM, 1968).

Patai, Raphael, *The Hebrew Goddess* (Detroit: Wayne State University Press, 1990^3).

Pritchard, James B (ed.), *The Ancient Near East: An Anthology of Texts and Pictures Volume 1* (Princeton: Princeton University Press, 1958).

Rad, Gerhard von, *Genesis: A Commentary* (SCM, 1961).

Rad, Gerhard von, *Old Testament Theology Volume 1: The Theology of Israel's Historical Traditions* (London: SCM, 1975).

Rad, Gerhard von, *Old Testament Theology Volume 2: The Theology of Israel's Prophetic Traditions* (London: SCM, 1965).

Rogerson, John and Davies, Philip R, *The Old Testament World* (London: T & T Clark International, 2005).

Snaith, Norman H, *Notes on the Hebrew Text of Genesis I – VIII* (London: Epworth Press, 1947).

Snaith, Norman H, *Notes on the Hebrew Text of Jeremiah, Chapters III, VII and XXXI* (London: Epworth Press, 1945).

Snaith, Norman H, *Notes on the Hebrew Text of 1 Kings XVII – XIX and XXI – XXII* (London: Epworth Press, 1954).

Soggin, J Alberto, *A History of Israel: From the Beginnings to the Bar Kochba Revolt, AD 135* (London: SCM, 1984).

Soggin, J Alberto, *Joshua* (London: SCM, 1972).

Soggin, J Alberto, *Judges* (London: SCM, 1987[2]).

Vaux, Roland de, *Ancient Israel: Its Life and Institutions* (London: Darton, Longman & Todd, 1965[2]).

Vaux, Roland de, *The Early History of Israel to the Exodus and the Covenant of Sinai* (London: Darton, Longman & Todd, 1978).

White, Lynn T, *Machina ex Deo: Essays in the Dynamism of Western Culture* (Cambridge MA: Massachusetts Institute of Technology, 1968).

Williams, Jean M and Cox, Zachary, *The Gods Within: The Pagan Pathfinders Book of God and Goddess Evocations* (London: Moondust Books, 2008).

Moon Books invites you to begin or deepen your encounter with Paganism, in all its rich, creative, flourishing forms.